JESUS

AND

ISLAM

وَمَا أَنتَ عَلَيْنَا بِعَزِيزٍ قَالَ يَاقَوْمِ أَرَهْطِي أَعَزُّ عَلَيْكُم مِّنَ اللَّهِ وَاتَّخَذْتُمُوهُ
وَرَآءَكُمْ ظِهْرِيًّا إِنَّ رَبِّي بِمَا تَعْمَلُونَ مُحِيطٌ • وَيَاقَوْمِ اعْمَلُوا عَلَىٰ مَكَانَتِكُمْ
إِنِّي عَامِلٌ سَوْفَ تَعْلَمُونَ مَن يَأْتِيهِ عَذَابٌ يُخْزِيهِ وَمَنْ هُوَ كَاذِبٌ
وَارْتَقِبُوا إِنِّي مَعَكُمْ رَقِيبٌ • وَلَمَّا جَاءَ أَمْرُنَا نَجَّيْنَا شُعَيْبًا وَالَّذِينَ
آمَنُوا مَعَهُ بِرَحْمَةٍ مِّنَّا وَأَخَذَتِ الَّذِينَ ظَلَمُوا الصَّيْحَةُ فَأَصْبَحُوا فِي
دِيَارِهِمْ جَاثِمِينَ كَأَن لَّمْ يَغْنَوْا فِيهَا أَلَا بُعْدًا لِّمَدْيَنَ كَمَا بَعِدَتْ ثَمُودُ
وَلَقَدْ أَرْسَلْنَا مُوسَىٰ بِآيَاتِنَا وَسُلْطَانٍ مُّبِينٍ إِلَىٰ فِرْعَوْنَ وَمَلَئِهِ
فَاتَّبَعُوا أَمْرَ فِرْعَوْنَ وَمَا أَمْرُ فِرْعَوْنَ بِرَشِيدٍ • يَقْدُمُ قَوْمَهُ يَوْمَ
الْقِيَامَةِ فَأَوْرَدَهُمُ النَّارَ وَبِئْسَ الْوِرْدُ الْمَوْرُودُ وَأُتْبِعُوا فِي هَذِهِ
لَعْنَةً وَيَوْمَ الْقِيَامَةِ بِئْسَ الرِّفْدُ الْمَرْفُودُ ذَلِكَ مِنْ أَنبَاءِ الْقُرَىٰ
نَقُصُّهُ عَلَيْكَ مِنْهَا قَائِمٌ وَحَصِيدٌ وَمَا ظَلَمْنَاهُمْ وَلَكِن ظَلَمُوا
أَنفُسَهُمْ فَمَا أَغْنَتْ عَنْهُمْ آلِهَتُهُمُ الَّتِي يَدْعُونَ مِن دُونِ اللَّهِ مِن
شَيْءٍ لَّمَّا جَاءَ أَمْرُ رَبِّكَ وَمَا زَادُوهُمْ غَيْرَ تَتْبِيبٍ وَكَذَلِكَ

Jesus

AND

Islam

Douglas Jacoby

Postscript by
Abdel Aziz Sarah

JESUS AND ISLAM

ISBN: 978-1-958723-95-1. Printed in the United States of America.

Unless otherwise indicated, all Scripture references are from the *Holy Bible, New International Version*, copyright ©1973, 1978, 1984, 2011 by Biblica, Inc. Used by permission. All rights reserved worldwide.

Interior book design: Toney C. Mulhollan.

Cover design: Roy Applesamy.

Illumination Publishers titles may be purchased in bulk for classroom instruction, business, fund-raising, or sales promotional use. For information, please e-mail paul.ipibooks@me.com.

Illumination Publishers cares deeply about using renewable resources and uses recycled paper whenever possible.

Published by Illumination Publishers, www.ipibooks.com.

About the author: Since 2003, Dr. Douglas Jacoby has been a freelance teacher and consultant. With degrees from Duke, Harvard, and Drew, he has written more than thirty books, recorded over 1000 podcasts, and spoken in 125 nations around the world. Douglas is also professor of theology at Lincoln Christian University. In *Jesus and Islam*, he digs deep to share both biblically and personally from his first four decades as a follower of Christ. For more about the work and ministry of Douglas Jacoby go to www.douglasjacoby.com.

Inside title page: Leaf from manuscript of Qur'an, circa 1780.

ILLUMINATION PUBLISHERS **ip** www.ipibooks.com

CONTENTS

Contents

Acknowledgements

Thanks are due to Gwen Wichman, who transcribed the book from the original lecture series; Elizabeth Thompson, my chief proofreader and editor; Jerri Newman, Amy Morgan and Curt Simmons, also skilled and sensitive proofreaders; Echo Garrett, for many invaluable suggestions; and Toney Mulhollan, long-time friend and colleague in publishing.

Next, I am deeply appreciative to my friend Abdel Aziz Sarah for contributing the postscript. He is living proof that the gospel is for "every nation, tribe, people, and language" (Revelation 7:9).

Yet no one deserves more thanks, for her constant support through joy and sorrow, sickness and health, than my wife. She is a true jewel. Thank you, Vicki, for our first forty years.

Preface

I realize that readers of *Jesus and Islam* hail from a variety of backgrounds, and may have a number of reasons for taking the time to study this book.

- Maybe you know nothing about Islam, and this volume is your first introduction to the religion.
- Or perhaps, at the other end of the spectrum, you have taken a university-level class on Islam and seek to expand your knowledge.
- Maybe you are a Westerner who is apprehensive about Islam. You worry about what is going to happen to this world, and this fear has impelled you to increase your understanding.
- Or perhaps you are a Muslim. You follow the Qur'an, and have purchased this book out of personal interest. I am sure you will be reading with a critical eye to see if what I say is fair. I hope you will feel free to send any input, whether personal reflections or suggestions for future editions.

Regardless of your background or religion, my hope and prayer are that *Jesus and Islam* will stimulate every reader to deeper thought—and even some soul-searching.

But my goal is more than *stimulation*. Otherwise we might end up only confirming our own preconceived ideas. As psychologist William James once said, "A great many people think they are thinking when they are merely rearranging their prejudices." The first goal of this book is *education*. And with education comes responsibility.

The second, and loftier, goal of this book is *transformation*. For those of us who are Christians, doubtless the majority of my readers, we are called to honestly open the Scriptures and ask ourselves how well we are representing Christ to our Muslim neighbors. After all, how would *Jesus* relate to them? What would *he* say and do? To say we have room for improvement is a gross understatement. Too many of us have conformed to worldly ways in our prejudices and behaviors.

It is time to be transformed.

Douglas Jacoby

The Challenge:
Open Your Eyes

*These are the days when the Christian is
expected to praise every creed except his own.*
—G.K. Chesterton

The Middle East: the land of pyramids and ancient civilizations, oil and conflict, romantic legend and fierce religion; the Holy Land for Jews, Christians, and Muslims alike. During my travels to the region, I am always awed by the breathtaking view from the airplane window—stunning rock formations, mountains, rivers, plains, vast oceans of sand—an alien yet awesome vista. But I am equally awed by the region's rich and dynamic history.

Our study begins not in the Arabia of the twenty-first century, but in the Arabia of the seventh. The year is 610 AD. Muhammad believes the angel Gabriel has a message for him, and is imparting revelations in the cave of Hira'. Muhammad claims to be the last prophet of Allah—his special messenger to the Jews, Christians, and polytheists. The revelations are recorded, and a small band of men gathers round.

Now fast-forward fourteen hundred years. The band of men is no longer small, nor is it confined to the sands and rocks of Arabia. This has become one of the largest and most widespread religions on the planet—the second largest, in fact.

Nearly One in Four

This is the story of Islam, its sacred book, and the issues confronting every one of us as we give this world religion the consideration it is due. As the book progresses, we will address the difficulties of Christian-Muslim relations. Yet at the outset, my aim is to sound a call to understand, a challenge to think and broaden horizons.

Islam, after all, often dominates the news. In truth, Islam has been in the news for decades, particularly as Islamic political entities have influenced the West. Opinions abound concerning Islam and Muslim beliefs, and yet—so often the case with opinion and rumor—they are based more on prejudice than on fact. So many opinions, so little knowledge.

You may be tempted to think: What does all of this have to do with me? I live on the other side of the world. I'm never likely to visit Arabia or learn Arabic. How does Islam affect my life? Does it really matter?

Lest you disregard the Muslim faith, let me present a staggering fact—one that comes as a shock to some. **Nearly one in four human beings is a Muslim.** Not *will* be a Muslim or *has been* a Muslim, but *is one right now!* This means that fully twenty-four percent of mankind belongs to the Islamic faith. And the number is growing. Some experts predict that Muslims will outnumber Christians by 2050.

Most of us, sociologists say, have a social circle of about five hundred persons. Obviously, we do not know many of those people well, but we recognize all of them. We work together, study together, or are related by blood or by marriage. Perhaps we are neighbors, or our paths have crossed by pure happenstance. Five hundred is a lot of people. Imagine that our circle of friends and acquaintances were truly representative of the planet, proportionately and demographically. That would translate to twenty percent of our five hundred acquaintances, or *one hundred persons*, being Muslims!

We could hardly pretend not to care about their thoughts and habits, their views and behavior, since we could scarcely avoid all one hundred acquaintances. Every day, in fact, we would have multiple conversations and reminders of their existence. We wouldn't, we couldn't "play dumb." We would be forced, at the very least, to make an effort to understand their beliefs and their way of life.

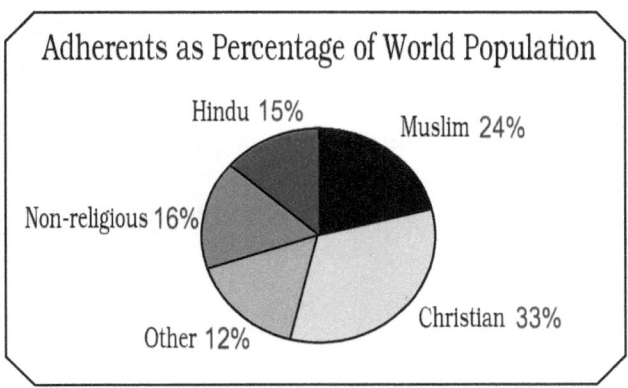

Adherents as Percentage of World Population

Hindu 15%
Muslim 24%
Non-religious 16%
Other 12%
Christian 33%

The Middle East?

Many Westerners have the impression that Muslims live only in the Middle East (Southwest Asia) and speak Arabic. This thinking reveals our ignorance and tendency to stereotype. Most Muslims do not call the Middle East home; rather, they live in the other parts of Asia—countries like Turkey, India, and Indonesia—or on the continent of Africa.

A huge number of nations boast extensive Muslim populations. The largest Islamic nation on the earth is Indonesia, with 230 million adherents. Muslims represent eighty-five to ninety percent of Indonesia's population. Indonesia is followed by India. Although its population is predominately Hindu, India still has more than 170 million Muslims—accounting for fifteen percent of its national population. Similarly, the country of Bangladesh has a population of about 150 million Muslims—ninety-eight percent of the nation. These nations are followed by Pakistan, Nigeria, Iran, Turkey, and Egypt.

As these statistics reveal, Muslims live all over the world, not just in the Middle East. Their influence encompasses a huge area, stretching from westernmost Africa all the way to the Philippines; from central Asia—exotic nations like Kazakhstan and Tajikistan—to European countries like Bosnia and Albania.

As a result of their varied national origins, most Muslims (eighty percent) do not speak Arabic. For example, Iranians do not speak Arabic, although their nation has a Muslim majority; Iranians speak Farsi and Persian. Islam is the official religion of Turkey, and yet the Turkish people do not speak Arabic, but Turkish. The same holds true of the Indonesians, who speak Bahasa. Arabic, in fact, is spoken only in parts of the Middle East and North Africa.

Persistent Stereotypes

But if most Muslims do not live in the Middle East or read the Qur'an in Arabic, why are we in the West usually confused about these facts? Why do the generalizations persist? If we are honest, we must acknowledge that the stereotypes extend beyond just national origin and language, covering such controversial issues as violence, fanaticism and misogyny. What factors have fostered and spread these enduring perceptions?

The answer is simple. The misinformation was borne out of centuries of ill will, antipathy, and even deliberate misrepresentation. I have just mentioned a few wrong notions about Muslims, but many more exist. Most Christians have probably mistakenly accepted at least some of these fallacies as true. We Christians have often held strong opinions about

Islam—many of them negative—but have seldom done our homework. Indeed, the Christian tendency to emphasize the dark side of Islam does no credit to Christianity, especially in light of the shameful deeds perpetuated against humanity under the banner of the Cross. In the words of an Arab proverb: "The tongue should have three gatekeepers: Is it true? Is it kind? Is it necessary?"[1]

Many Americans have been told that the Qur'an prophesied the "War on Terror" against Saddam Hussein and Osama bin Laden. Here is an email sent to me more than once in recent years:

> *"No other nation, except Israel, has more history and prophecy associated with it than Iraq... Since America is typically represented by an eagle, Saddam should have read up on his Muslim passages. The following verse is from the Koran (the Islamic Bible) 9:11—'For it is written that a son of Arabia would awaken a fearsome Eagle. The wrath of the Eagle would be felt throughout the lands of Allah and lo, while some of the people trembled in despair still more rejoiced; for the wrath of the Eagle cleansed the lands of Allah; and there was peace.' Note the verse number. It is 9:11. Hmm... God bless you all. Amen!"*

How easy it is for rumor and gossip to proliferate when no one bothers to check the facts! Sura 9, aya[2] 11 of the Qur'an says nothing of the sort mentioned above! The "prophecy" was concocted. Unfortunately, this hoax continues to make the rounds.

The real 9:11 reads: "But if they repent and pay the poor tax, they are brothers in faith. And we make the messages clear for a people who know." The text has nothing to do with an eagle or a cleansing. In fact, the word *eagle* does not even appear in the Qur'an! So much for the prophecy about America.

The lesson: Don't believe everything you read. Especially

things written to stir up enmity. The peoples of the Middle East are *not* my enemy. As the Bible says, "For our warfare is not against flesh and blood" (Ephesians 6:12).

And yet enmity *is* being stirred up. Those who misrepresent Islam *are* affecting the public. A recent U.S. Gallup Poll revealed that twenty-two percent of Americans would not want a Muslim as a neighbor, and fewer than fifty percent believe American Muslims are loyal to the United States.[3] It doesn't help matters any that prominent religious leaders have demonized Muslims. The late Jerry Falwell called Muhammad "a terrorist." Pat Robertson called him "an absolute wild-eyed fanatic... a robber and brigand... a killer." Even Franklin Graham (son of Billy Graham) described Islam as "a very evil and very wicked religion."

Having encouraged civility and fairness, I feel the need to make one important qualification. Being fair in our investigation of Islam does not require us to accept it as somehow true. If we did, honesty would dictate that we *convert!* As C.S. Lewis aptly remarked: "If Christianity is untrue, then no honest man will want to believe it, however helpful it might be: if it is true, every honest man will want to believe it, even if it gives him no help at all."[4] Integrity dictates that we follow the truth wherever it leads us. Our inquiry does not require that we pretend to ourselves, or to anyone else, that we are wrong and the other fellow is right.

Malaysia, Moustafa and Me

My first direct experience with Islam goes back to university days, when I first read the Qur'an cover-to-cover. Four years later, I made my first trip to a Muslim nation, spending a full month in the nation of Malaysia (a country between Singapore—just one degree above the equator—and Thailand). The *muezzins* broadcast the customary prayers just a hundred meters from the home in which I stayed. That visit also gave me my first opportunity to set foot inside a mosque. Nearly every year since, I have visited a mosque somewhere in the world. I have generally found the imams and worshipers civil, if not helpful, to their foreign guests.

I lived in London for eight years, and there I had my first chance to get to know a "real Muslim"—an Egyptian by the name of Moustafa. Like me, he was in his early twenties, full of life and confidence. He showed me his prayer rug, and explained how deeply he believed in Allah. His entire life centered round his religious convictions.

We cultivated a relationship of mutual respect—even admiration—through shared meals and frank discussions. We were honest, talking openly about our lives and our faith. I was amazed by how much Moustafa and I had in common. In a way, I saw myself in him, and him in me: different faiths, different upbringings, yet linked by a common passion for our distinct religions. In fact, each of us was trying to convert the other! Yet our commonality was not unbounded. Our religions could hardly have been more different.

What impressed me about Moustafa was his sincerity, his obvious belief in Allah, and his desire to persuade me that his faith was true. He wanted to convince me about the truth of Islam just as much as I wanted to convince him about the truth of Jesus Christ!

Since that time in 1983 I have interacted privately with scores, perhaps hundreds, of Muslims. My first *public* interactions with members of the Islamic faith took place in Europe in the mid-1980s. Often as I gave public presentations, I would have some friendly banter with the audience. Although these interactions would sometimes turn into a debate, they were usually quite civil. Unlike many Christians, who are "Christian" merely in a cultural sense, many of the Muslims who came to my lectures were passionate about their beliefs.

I have logged millions of miles traveling the world as an international speaker, specializing in the Bible. I have spoken with Muslims in Europe and Africa, and all over Asia and in the Middle East. I have been welcomed into their homes, studied the Bible with them, and even baptized some of them as

Christians. I was even privileged to observe the "Arab Spring" from inside the Middle East, including four exciting days in Cairo (days two to four of the protest). I have found Muslims to be little different from most other people on the planet.

While I do not subscribe to their religion, I always strive to treat Muslims with the utmost respect. Yes, I know the stereotypes—but I also know many Muslims.

Modern Pluralism

Our society is increasingly pluralistic. We are exposed to a broad spectrum of world views, not just one. Not so long ago, in traditional society, and even in my own country, the United States, most people lived in communities with little diversity. The religious options might have been, say, Methodist versus Baptist, Church of Christ versus Catholic. But let's face it: From an outsider's perspective, these Christian denominations all have a lot in common. (Oh yes, there might have been a synagogue here and there, but that was about as exotic as things got in the United States of America.)

Today, not just in major metropolitan areas, but often even in midsize cities, we find unprecedented pluralism. In some towns, on a short drive we could easily pass a variety of Christian churches, as well as mosques and temples of Buddhists, Hindus, Jains, and Sikhs.

This intermingling of ideas and beliefs has, for better or worse, caused many of us to question our fundamental assumptions. Is our faith perspective right? Is our religion true? What if we are wrong? Do we believe for merely environmental reasons—that is, because we were brought up in a particular religious environment—or do we have solid reasons to believe as we do?

Tolerance False and True

Rather than search out honest answers to these difficult questions, many people opt for the easy way out. They adopt the popular, politically correct attitude that is falsely called "tolerance."[5] "I'm a modern, educated person," they say with a self-satisfied smile, "and so I tolerate all people, all beliefs, all religions. I don't judge others—can't we all just get along?"

But often this "tolerance" is just mental laziness. What they are *really* saying is, "I don't want to study and think and compare, so I prefer to believe all religions are true." And so they blindly embrace a dominant cultural myth of our times: All roads lead to God, and as long as you are a sincere person, you will find him/her/it in your own way. That is a lovely idea, but a myth. Indeed, if the Bible is true, most roads lead away from God. In our eagerness not to offend, we gloss over major religious differences, pretending we all agree, when in fact our points of *agreement* are only superficial.

An analogy may help. You have heard it said, "All roads lead to Rome." I am sure that to an ancient Roman, living in that Mediterranean city of one million people—the largest city in the western world—it might well have appeared that all roads led to Rome. But of course, that would only have been a subjective viewpoint.

To modernize the illustration, do all planes land at Rome's Leonardo da Vinci-Fiumicino Airport? Not at all. Or Chicago's O'Hare International Airport? It might seem that way if you live in Chicago—especially if you live under the flight path. But then, the same would seem true for someone whose local airport is Los Angeles, Atlanta, London, Frankfurt, Hong Kong, or Singapore. Planes fly a myriad of complex routes. Just as claiming that all planes land in Chicago sounds simple-minded, so asserting that all the religions of the world somehow end up in the same place—at heaven's doorstep—is both wishful and simplistic.

Some naively think that, as long as we call our god "God," we are all worshiping the same being.[6] "You see," they say, "we all worship God in our own way." But as the apostle Paul argued in Acts 17, if we are worshipping out of ignorance, we need to be corrected.

To begin with, not all people call their god "God." The

Muslims call him *Allah*. Spanish speakers say *Dios*. In Eastern Europe, many say *Bog*. With my upbringing in the United States, I say *God*. There are hundreds of names for God, and thousands of gods,[7] but even if everyone did utilize the same word, "God," why should we assume we're all praying to the same being? What defines a god, after all, isn't the *name* of the deity, but his (or her) *nature*. On this register the deities of the world vary widely.

Let's not allow fuzzy thinking in the name of "tolerance"[8] to blind us to the real differences among religions. After all, as someone put it, "Tolerance gets a lot of credit that belongs to apathy."

> To claim that Islam and Christianity basically teach the same thing is to deliberately ignore points of doctrine considered sacred and nonnegotiable by both parties.

Evaluating World Religions

When considering the world religions, we have to look at *content*, not just terminology or external trappings. We must examine what the religions themselves teach, resisting the temptation to assume that everyone sees the same things we do. Most people believe in something—perhaps a god or gods, or self, or good luck, or "the Force" (of *Star Wars* fame). But claiming that all these beings or concepts are one and the same doesn't make sense.

For example, Krishna is not the god who gave the Law to Moses. Buddha is not the god we read about in the Bible. In fact, the evidence shows that the historical Buddha was an atheist. "The Force" did not die on the cross for us.

If Christianity is true, God became flesh. This concept is called the incarnation, an idea that is anathema to Muslims, who are scandalized by the teaching that Jesus was God in the flesh. Since the incarnation is a central teaching of the Christian faith, to claim that Islam and Christianity basically teach the same thing is to deliberately ignore points of doctrine considered sacred and nonnegotiable by both parties. Such generalizations are not only inaccurate; they are also unfair, even insulting.

> Most experts... agree that the differences among religions strikingly outweigh the similarities.

We have to ask some tough questions as we compare the various religions. Similarities surface at first blush, of course, but they are superficial: faith in a higher power, conformity to a certain code, visits to places of worship, or the practice of meditation. Many prescribe meetings and promise certain privileges for the adherents. But note that these descriptions would apply to almost any human group or organization! They would apply to service groups, to the Scouts, to many university clubs.

In fact, the experts—those who actually study the various belief systems across the entire human religious spectrum—agree that the differences among religions strikingly outweigh the similarities.[9]

To make a legitimate analysis, we have to examine the differences in key areas, such as the overall concept of God, the standard of what is right and wrong, and the way followers relate to other people. We should ask questions about relationships, ethics and morality, questions like: What does it take to be committed in this religion? What does this religion's god expect? What is the ultimate goal? Where does everything lead? In all these areas, the world religions are violently opposed.

The Challenge
With all these things in mind, we can begin our examination of the Muslim faith with a proper mindset. I hope that by now

you are willing to shed assumptions you may have wrongly held, and that you are ready to take a fresh, unfettered look at Islam and its teachings.

This book will stretch you. The challenge of understanding Islam is immense. Specifically, this book will push you to:

- Expand your horizons.
- Shed sentimentality and learn to think critically.
- Master the basics of Islam.
- Appreciate your own faith.
- Look at Muslims through the eyes of Christ.
- Connect with one-fifth of mankind.

In these pages, I share not just my experience and observations, but also the fruit of my study of the Qur'an—along with the convictions formed by observing current events in recent decades.

And so let us begin our exploration of the Islamic faith, examining its origins and founder, scriptures and doctrines, including its penchant for violence. The book will conclude with suggestions on how we can connect with Muslims. The intellectual and spiritual journey will not be easy, but will be well worth the effort.

Let us open our eyes! Let us accept the challenge.

2

Islam from 622 to the Present Day

There must be something in [Islam] itself to explain
its persistence and spread, and to account for its
present hold over so large of a proportion of the
dwellers on the earth... Islam has stirred an
enthusiasm that has never been surpassed.
— Ali Unal, author and political editorialist

As we have learned, one in five human beings today is a Muslim. Out of a world population approaching seven billion, 1.4 billion live under the Crescent! Islam is the world's second largest religion. And yet it is hardly an ancient faith. Many express surprise when they learn that it is one of the world's youngest faiths.

The genesis of Islam in Arabia took place in the 600s AD. Much like the world we live in today, Arabia at that time was a pluralistic society playing host to a number of different faiths.

The majority of Arabians were polytheistic, worshiping a multiplicity of gods.[10] Most popular were the sun and the moon. Some considered the moon the chief god. (The moon was usually viewed as male, while the sun was female.) But monotheistic faiths also thrived in the Arabian Peninsula. In fact, a reading of the Qur'an indicates that Muhammad was well acquainted with both Jews and Christians, specifically Catholic Christians.[11] Moreover, there were also Zoroastrians[12] and Manichees[13] in Arabia, not to mention animists of various kinds.

Muhammad took issue with the idolatry, greed, oppression, and hypocrisy rampant among the Arabians and their many religions. Like the Old Testament prophets, he correctly saw the link between wrong theology and immoral behavior. Worship the wrong god, and there are consequences. Muhammad boldly spoke out, and his words are now preserved in the Qur'an.

How did he make others believe that he was God's messenger? How did he become the prophet for this new religion? He must have been a convincing person, persuading others of his honesty, conviction, or chances of success.

In 610 AD, when he was forty years old, Muhammad claimed that the angel Gabriel spoke to him. Gabriel told Muhammad that he was called to be the prophet of a new faith—and yet not a completely new religion, since Muhammad affirmed that Islam was a natural continuation of the great faiths that had preceded it, first Judaism and then Christianity. Muhammad said that Noah was a Muslim, as were Abraham, Isaac, Ishmael, Jacob, David, Solomon, and a multitude of other well-known biblical figures.

Jesus was a prophet—the greatest, in fact, until the last prophet: Muhammad himself. Gabriel relayed Allah's message to Muhammad, charging him to call people to repent, to worship the one God, to turn away from idolatry, to renounce social injustice, and to embrace truth. A biblical Christian would not object to most of these messages.

Initially, Muhammad and his men tried to persuade the people of Mecca, his hometown. But despite their best attempts, they were rejected. So they fled to Medina in 622 AD, the year which Muslims date as the beginning of their religion. Seventy men and their families went ahead of the prophet to Medina.[14] This flight is called the *hijrah*.[15] In Medina the Muslims were able to flourish.[16]

From this point on, the method of extending the Islamic faith took a violent turn. Not to say that all who embraced Islam did so under duress. That would be an unfair misrepresentation of the historical truth. In fact, sura 2:256 reads, "There is no compulsion in religion..." Studies show that many of Islam's early (monotheistic) allies did not convert. Still, violence figured prominently in the defense and spread of the fledgling faith, especially with each passing century.

Year AD	Hijrah Year
622	1
1000	244
1500	905
1900	1317
2000	1421
2020	1441

Scholars agree that before Muhammad and his men began to employ violence as a tactic, the expansion of the faith was minimal, and probably discouraging. Revelations permitting warfare paved the way for the new strategy. Not surprisingly, once they took up the sword, the number of Muslim followers began to burgeon rapidly.

The Qur'an clearly teaches that Muslims may defend themselves militarily, and authorizes them to fight those infidels who oppose Allah and his messengers. Once Muslims took up the sword, many were converted.

A Religion of Submission

Muhammad called everyone to worship one god, and he claimed to be the prophet of that one god. The call, even today, is to *submit*. Not just to submit to Muhammad, but to Allah, the god of Islam. This is the meaning of *islam*, the Arabic word for submission.

In an apparent effort to make the religion more appealing and politically correct, some people—those who I doubt have studied Arabic—claim that *Islam* means "peace." But the Arabic word *salaam* (Hebrew shalom) is the word for *peace*. Of course there may be an etymological connection between the words salaam and islam, somewhere in the past. But even if this is true, that still does not change the meaning of the word *islam*, or its usage.

For example, the English *butterfly* is a strange word. I am sure that *butter* and *fly* came together for some reason,[17] but to opine that a butterfly has something to do with butter is wishful thinking at best! Let's not play those kinds of semantic games.

Islam means submission, pure and simple. This is the essence of the faith. In terms of submission to this faith, many people, tribes, and even entire nations have submitted, for Islam spread through political, economic, and military channels. Those who refused to submit soon found themselves at a significant disadvantage.

What's in a Name?

Do you know what the most common name in the world is? One might suppose that it is *John*. This ubiquitous man's name appears, of course, in various other forms: *Jan, Johann, Owen, Ian,* and so forth. Those all go back to the original Greek name for John, *Ioannes.* Counting all its permutations, John seems a likely pick for world's commonest name. But in fact it isn't. The honor goes to *Muhammad.*

Muhammad too has variant forms, like Ahmed, Mehmet, Mahmud, Hamid, and others. (Every nation, every dialect has different variants.) All variants considered, the plurality of babies born in the world are *Muhammads.*

But was Muhammad just a man?

Some Variations of Muhammad:	
Achmad	Mehdi
Achmet	Mehmed
Ahmad	Mehmet
Ahmed	Mohamed
Hamid	Mohamet
Mahmood	Mohammad
Mahmud	Mohammed
Mahomet	Muhammed

Muhammad: Perfect Man or Divinity?

Since he is so revered, let us take a closer look at Muhammad, the founder of the Islamic faith. Given the slender evidence in the Qur'an, today we may be too far away from the time of Muhammad to psychoanalyze him, or to assess such attributes as anger or humility. Though most Muslims claim he was illiterate,[18] we do know that he was a man of formidable power.

At first Muhammad attacked caravans, then cities, and within a few decades, empires were bowing before the god of Islam. One reason the efforts at conversion succeeded was a political power vacuum: the Persian and Byzantine Empires had depleted themselves through their many wars. Muhammad was a strong leader, tolerant at times but stern at others. He even had some of his opponents assassinated for mocking him in their poems.[19]

Muhammad claimed to be "the seal of the prophets" (33:40), the last and greatest of a long succession reaching back through Jesus, Moses, and Abraham, all the way to Adam. He warned that whoever failed to heed his message would pay for it in eternity.

> Know they not that whoever opposes Allah and His
> Messenger, for him is the Fire of hell to abide in it? That
> is the grievous abasement. —Qur'an 9:63

Although Muhammad claims to be a human, not a divinity, his followers speak of him with a reverence far surpassing mere respect. For example, he is called "Lord of the Universe." Many Muslims also call him "Savior of the World."[20] Most followers, when his name is mentioned, will say, "Peace be upon him," or, if they are writing in English, "PBUH." Savior of the World, Lord of the Universe—these epithets show the kind of respect we would give to God.

Muslims believe that Muhammad made his night journey upon the flying steed Buraq, the traditional heavenly steed of the prophets, brought to him by the archangel Gabriel at the Sacred Mosque in Mecca in 621 AD. It is reported in sura 17:1 of the Qu'ran, with more details in the *Hadith* (tradition), that he was first flown by Buraq from the mosque in Mecca to the "farthest mosque" in the holy city of Jerusalem, the part of the trip called the *isra*. After a brief stop to pray, Buraq then launched his master from the place memorialized by the Dome of the Rock, up through the seven circles, or levels, of heaven. This second part of the trip is known as the *mi'r'aj*. While in heaven he talked with the prophets of old, including Moses, Abraham, John the Baptist, and Jesus, and, finally, after receiving instructions directly from *Allah* about how to pray, (five, not three, times a day), he is returned by Buraq to Mecca. Some Muslims interpret this as a vision, others as a literal journey.

And yet the facts of history, coupled with the claims of the Qur'an itself, indicate that Muhammad was more earthly than these exalted claims and stories might suggest. To use biblical terminology, he was (like you and me) a "sinner." Of course, I would not advise you to parachute into Saudi Arabia and hold up an Arabic sign proclaiming, "Muhammad was a sinner." Yet controversial (to a Muslim) as this statement may be, it is based upon the Qur'an itself. Let us examine two verses confirming Muhammad's sinfulness. In sura 40 we read the following instructions from Allah to Muhammad:

> Patiently, then, persevere: For the promise of Allah is true: and ask forgiveness for your fault... (Qur'an[21] 40:55).

A few suras later we read:
> Know, therefore, that there is no God but God, and ask forgiveness for your fault, and for the men and women who believe... (47:19)

Here we find texts clearly indicating that Muhammad himself needed to seek forgiveness. These passages should not surprise us, since we are ordinary, flawed mortals, but they are highly problematic for Muslims, many of whom believe that all of Allah's prophets were sinless (Jesus included).[22]

Over time, Muhammad has become *virtually* deified. And this even though Muslims are strict monotheists! (Again, if you parachute into Mecca holding a sign that reads, "Muhammad is God," you will land in deep trouble.) But this veneration is not just a phenomenon within the Muslim religion—it is a common feature of world religions. Once the founder has died, his status is greatly exalted.

The Buddha instructed his disciples not to worship him after he was gone.[23] But what happened? After Buddha died, people began worshiping him and praying to him. I've seen people praying to statues of the Buddha all over the world, particularly in Asia. The same happened to Confucius. He did not even claim to be a good man,[24] and yet he is widely worshiped today. Every religion evolves—including Hinduism, Christianity, Sikhism, Judaism—and the same is certainly true of Islam.

Despite the fact that the Qur'an says that Muhammad was a sinner, he is now treated with a reverence that is worthy of God alone.

But what, specifically, did this venerated man teach? What kind of requirements and lifestyle did he expect of his followers? Now that we have taken a look at the founder of Islam, let us proceed to examining the religion's central tenets.

The Five Pillars

The Qur'an contains the five basic teachings of Islam, called the five pillars. Upon these five pillars the structure of Islam rests.

> ## The Five Pillars of Islam
>
> Confession
> Almsgiving
> Prayer
> Fasting
> Pilgrimage

The first pillar is *shahadah*, or confession. What is the confession that Muslims make? It is a humble and obedient admission that there is but one God and that Muhammad is the prophet of God. If you sincerely utter the shahadah—and this obviously rules out believing in Jesus as God—then you are a Muslim. That is what Islam teaches.

> Shahadah: *"Lā ilāha illāllah umuḥammadun rasulūllāh."*
> "There is no God but Allah and Muhammad is the messenger of Allah."

The second pillar is *zakat*, or almsgiving, giving to the poor. *Zakat* is not necessarily monetary. Payments might be made in camels, levied on the discovery of buried treasure, and so forth. There is a strong emphasis in Islam and in the Qur'an on helping the needy. As sura 9:60 reads: "*Zakat* is only for the poor and the needy, and those employed to administer it, and those whose hearts are made to incline (to truth), and (to free) the captives and those in debt, and in the way of Allah and for the wayfarer—an ordinance from Allah..." To this end, Muslims are asked to give one fortieth (two-and-a-half percent) of all liquid assets—not just their annual income.[25] Shi'ites, who constitute ten to fifteen percent of all Muslims, are expected to give away one fifth of their income.[26]

The third pillar is *salah*, or prayer. As sura 62:9 has it: "O you who believe, when the call is sounded for prayer on

Friday, hasten to the remembrance of Allah and leave off business. That is better for you, if you know." Prayer is preceded by
obligatory ritual washing.

When you read the Qur'an, you will see that Muslims are
called to pray three times a day (11:114; 13:15). This number
was later changed to five, although you will not see the altered
teaching in the Qur'an. The traditions of Islam, called the *Hadith*, determine how Muslims live, and if there is any discrep-
ancy with the Qur'an, the Hadith are authoritative.[27]

> "Wake up, wake up! Prayer is better than sleep."
> —Part of the call to *Fazur* (morning prayer).

While prayer may be performed anywhere, it is considered
as especially effective when done in community, in a mosque.[28]
Yet we should not think that Muslim prayer is the same as
Christian prayer. The principal part of Muslim prayer is worship, whereas the principal part of most Christian prayer is
supplication. That is, faithful Muslims acknowledge Allah's
lordship over the universe throughout the day, whereas many
Christians pray inconsistently, and even when they do, their
prayers are dominated by petitions for themselves. As Gerald
McDermott puts it: "Evangelicals can be reminded by Muslim practice that the heart of prayer is worship and that a
prayer life dominated by supplication is unbalanced and self-
absorbed. They can also learn from Muslims the importance
of regularity in prayer and how set times can help check our
inclination to forget about prayer entirely."[29]

When I visit Muslim nations; (like Albania, Bangladesh,
Turkey, Indonesia, and Guinea), I hear the public call to prayer
five times each day. It emanates from a *muezzin* standing in a
tower, his voice often amplified by a loudspeaker. All who hear
are supposed to bow and face Mecca, (the holiest city of Islam,
located in Saudi Arabia), and pray. In many countries, everyone stops what he is doing, falls to the ground, and repeats
the required words. I have even seen devout Muslims pull out
prayer rugs from the overhead compartments in airplanes and
prostrate themselves in the aisle!

> Surely man is created impatient—fretful when evil af-
> flicts him, And niggardly when good befalls him—ex-
> cept those who pray, who are constant at their prayer...
> —Qur'an 70:19–23

The fourth pillar is *sawm*, or fasting. Muslims fast during the month of Ramadan. The fast extends through the daylight hours. During the entire month, Muslims take no food or drink until sundown. (They are also to abstain from smoking, chewing gum, and marital relations.) In some countries, this type of fast is relatively easy. But imagine how it would be in places where heat and sand punish and dehydrate the body all day long. Under such conditions, it is far more challenging not to have any food or water. According to tradition, Muhammad said that of all the duties of a Muslim, *sawm* is most loved by Allah, since he alone sees it.

Having said that, however, the daytime *fast* is followed by a nighttime *feast*. It is common in Muslim nations for food sales to be greater during Ramadan than during any other month of the year! So the fasting period is a time not just of focusing on Allah, but also of joy and feasting in the evenings.

Ramadan is also a time for extra prayer, for giving alms to the poor, and devoting oneself to good works.

The fifth and final pillar is pilgrimage. Pilgrimage is called *hajj*, and one who goes on a pilgrimage is a *hajji*. The holy cities of Islam are Medina, Jerusalem, and Mecca. Muslims at first prayed towards Jerusalem (622 AD), but soon after changed to praying towards Mecca (624 AD).[30]

Pilgrimage is made to Mecca, and if you are physically—and financially—able to travel to Arabia, the holy city of Mecca, you must do this at least once in your lifetime. Pilgrims, clad in seamless white robes and strapless white shoes, visit the Great Mosque, home of the ancient black rock called the Kaaba, the meteorite that Muslims claim was visited by Abraham.[31]

Today, the Great Mosque is the most holy place in the Islamic world. Over two million throng Mecca annually during the traditional period of the Hajj. They walk counterclockwise seven times around the Kaaba, kissing it, and they perform many other rituals, including a symbolic stoning of the devil.

Those are the five pillars: confession, fasting, almsgiving, prayer, and pilgrimage. Some Muslims add a sixth pillar, and that is *jihad*. We will discuss jihad in greater detail in chapter four.

Branches of Islam

Building on these pillars, Islam spread out both geographically and doctrinally. That is to say, not all Muslims hold to the same teachings, although the basic doctrines are held in common.

Eighty-five percent of Muslims are *Sunnis*. They constitute the mainstream. The *Wahabi* sect is an important group within the Sunnis, strong and fundamentalist. The *Shi'ites*, who disagree with the Sunnis over the identity of the rightful successors of Muhammad, and who also focus more on the inner spiritual life than the Sunnis,[32] comprise the other fifteen percent of Muslims. Shi'ites are subdivided into such groups as *Zaidis, Imamis, Isma'ilis,* and *Ahmadiyyas.*

> "Prayer carries us halfway to God; fasting brings us to the door of his praises; almsgiving grants us admission." —Muslim proverb

We could go down one more level, because these major groupings can be subdivided. This is the nature of religion—to fracture because of disagreements.[33]

One of the most colorful movements within Islam, well-known in the West, is Sufism. Sufi is a Muslim mystic. The Christians have had their mystics who would go into the wilderness and live alone, striving to commune with God. The Jews have those who follow the Kabala and seek mystical union with Yahweh. Likewise, the Muslims have the Sufis.[34]

The most famous Sufis are probably the Whirling Dervishes. They spin around and dance in ecstasy, striving for an altered state of consciousness during which they can commune with God. Some of them speak in tongues. Indeed, tongue-speaking, or *glossolalia*,[35] is a feature of Sufism, as it is of Pentecostalism, Mormonism, Shamanism and numerous ancient religions.

Denominations of Islam

Sunni (85-90%)	**Smaller groups**
Hanafi	Kharijite
Deobandi	• Azraqi
Maliki	• Ibadi
Shafi'i	• Surfri
Hanbali	Kalam
Wahabi	• Ash'ari
Salafi	• Jabriyya
	• Maturdi
Shi'ite (10-15%)	• Marjih
Zaidi	• Mu'tazilli
Imami	• Q'diriyyah
Isma'ili	
• Nizaris	**Sufi (mystics)**
• Musta'lis	Whirling dervishes
Ahmadiyya	Tongue-speakers
Jafari	Poets (often spiritualizing the
Alani	violent passages of scripture)
Alevi	

Expansion

The Muslim faith has spread around the world, with a geographical expansion nothing short of stunning. Recall that

Islam began in Arabia in the early 600s. Within a century, Islam was established from India in the east, all the way to Tunisia in the west. It was even beginning to take over Europe. Before the 700s were over, there were Muslims in Spain—about 4600 kilometers (2850 miles) away from Mecca—and even more impressive, Spain had become a largely Muslim nation. A few centuries later we find *millions* of Muslims in India,[36] while in the west, Islam was making significant headway among the kingdoms of Europe.

It is amazing that within a hundred years, this empire, called the Caliphate (the territory controlled by the caliphs, or successors of Muhammad), had spread from Spain to India. Within a century, the Caliphate had become larger than the Roman Empire at its peak! (However, it was arguably less influential in the course of world history and culture.)

Eventually, Islam spread as far east as the Philippines (in the fourteenth century), and today, the Muslim faith is common in the southern Philippine islands.[37] Today there are fifty-seven nations with substantial or majority Muslim populations.

Islam cut an impressively broad swath across the earth. Why did it grow so rapidly? Why the great success?

Nature abhors a vacuum, spiritually speaking. Many of the countries where Islam flourished had no strong, vital religion. Arabia, at the time of Islam's birth, had a wide spectrum of religions, but no vibrant, dominant faith.

Judaism, Christianity, and the polytheistic Arabian religions all preceded Islam historically, yet in the seventh century these religions were morally bankrupt. People—most of whom probably claimed to be religious—lived in a worldly way. They cared about themselves; they loved money; they disregarded the poor. Although this is, perhaps, over generalizing, the widespread adoption of the Islamic faith, from then until now, cannot be disputed.

In the early years Muslims interacted with people of other faiths in relative peace. In fact, the earlier suras of the Qur'an, before tensions between Christians and Muslims became intractable, acknowledge that some of the Christians were living upright lives:

Surely those who believe, and those who are Jews, and the Christians, and the Sabeans, whoever believes in Allah and the Last Day and does good, they have their reward with their Lord, and there is no fear for them, nor shall they grieve (2:62).[38]

They are not all alike. Of the People of the Book there is an upright party who recite Allah's messages in the night-time and they adore (Him). They believe in Allah and the Last Day, and they enjoin good and forbid evil and vie with one another in good deeds. And those are among the righteous. And whatever good they do, they will not be denied it. And Allah knows those who keep their duty (3:112-114).[39]

But let us look at the big picture. The weakness of the religions of Asia—including Christianity, which at that time was soft and decadent, a far cry from the original faith—allowed Islam to spread into the vacuum all through Asia, Africa and Europe.

The Decadence of Christianity

I am not down on Christians—being one myself. However, there is a colossal difference between authentic Christianity and cultural Christianity. We who are Christians cannot condone all that has been done in the name of our faith, nor can we agree with everything that Christianity has become today. In the first hundred years of the faith, most Christians held to the biblical teachings wholeheartedly, often with a commitment unto death, but most of that changed in the fourth century. In the 300s, Christianity not only became legal and no longer subject to persecution, but it also became the official religion of the Roman Empire.

In no time, Christianity became a virtual prerequisite for

financial success. Pagans were ordered to report to churches for instruction and baptism; those who refused suffered confiscation of property and exile. Conformity was enforced, and those who refused to obey their new "Christian" leaders (pagans, Jews, and even Christians of different views) paid dearly. Millions were baptized, with little if any understanding of the meaning of the faith. At this point, the church went into tremendous decline.

As a teacher of church history, I explain that in the early 300s most people who claimed to follow Christ probably did. The fires of persecution periodically purified the church, and there was a high price to pay for leadership. Most churchgoers were authentic in their relationship with God. But by the later 300s, only a minority of those who went to church, and claimed the name of Christ, represented him in their lives. Three centuries later, in the 600s, we can only imagine how much more corrupt the faith had become. As the Islamic hordes spread, many Christians capitulated, promptly converting to the new religion.

Muslims did not always force the locals to convert; sometimes they gave a choice. Many Muslim leaders were fair men, and actually lived in a state of tolerance and peace with their Christian and Jewish neighbors. But in other places, ultimatums were issued, and many Christians submitted to the Crescent. For example, the Egyptian Christians weighed the pros and cons of converting to Islam, and for the majority—though not for the Coptic minority—the choice was straightforward. Life would be smoother under their new Muslim overlords if they cooperated.

Once again, by the time Muhammad was born in 570, Catholic Christianity had drifted far from its first-century moorings. It had made peace with the world, relaxed its high moral standards, developed a powerful priesthood, and made many more alterations that its humble founder would certainly have rejected. As Islam spread, it moved into a *moral* power vacuum. Even today, wherever Christianity remains anemic, Islam—or other vibrant faiths—will continue to rush in to fill the void.

> "He is Allah, besides whom there is no other god. He is the Sovereign Lord, the Holy One, the Giver of Peace, the Keeper of Faith; the Guardian, the Mighty One, the All-Powerful, the Most High! Exalted be He above their idols! He is Allah, the Creator, the Originator, the Modeler. His are the gracious names. All that is in heaven and earth gives glory to Him. He is the Mighty, the Wise One." —Qur'an 59:23-24

Motives for Conversion

Are there additional reasons that explain the rapidity of Islam's growth? Of course there are. The Western Roman Empire had virtually disintegrated. The Byzantine Empire, based in the new Rome (the city of Constantinople, modern-day Istanbul[40]) was weakening. This made the new movement more attractive. There were also economic benefits to becoming a Muslim. Muslims paid lower taxes and received favorable economic treatment from governors. They were less likely to be enslaved.

Considering that there were so many motives for conversion, analysis from so many centuries away is problematic. It seems probable that the primary reason that Islam spread so easily was the moral bankruptcy of the competition.

Today Islam continues to grow as much through its followers' high birthrates as through efforts to proselytize. This is especially true in Asia, Africa, and Southwest Asia (the Middle East). Islam does have its converts, but the number of converts is relatively small compared to the number of new Muslims who are born into the faith.

Nation of Islam?

If you live in North America, you may be wondering: What about the "millions" of Muslims in the United States? True, some western countries have significant Muslim minorities. For example, the Muslim population of the United Kingdom is approximately three percent.[41] In contrast, the United States actually has relatively few Muslims, probably no more than one percent of the total population.[42] The common estimate of six million practitioners is an exaggerated number, in part because it includes members of the group called the Nation of Islam.

But, you may ask, don't they count as Muslims? That depends on whom you ask. To illustrate, the Nation of Islam is generally viewed by Muslims worldwide in the same way that Mormonism is viewed by Christians. Christians do not claim that Mormons are *totally* wrong. A number of their teachings are biblical, and often we are impressed by their lives—particularly by their solidarity, community spirit, and families. But Mormonism includes many doctrines at odds with Scripture, and several of its practices are alien to the spirit of the Bible. In short, Christians do not see Mormonism as a movement representing authentic or mainstream Christianity; rather, it is a man-made and somewhat bizarre version of the faith.

This is more or less the same way that Muslims view the Nation of Islam. In fact, the Nation of Islam has been rejected by most Muslims around the world. One reason for this is that its membership is racially based.[43] It speaks primarily to African-Americans, and much less to those outside that ethnic group. The Nation of Islam also holds to a number of doctrines that do not make sense in terms of the Qur'an and classical Islam.[44]

The Contributions of Islam

What has Islam brought to the world? We do no justice to the faith by focusing only on negative aspects, or present-day concerns about global terrorism. To be fair, Islam has brought multiple blessings to the world, beginning with the elegant Arabic language. Hundreds of familiar English words have

Arabic roots, including *admiral, alcove, alkali, apricot, assassin, azure, camel, candy, cipher, coffee, cotton, guitar, hazard, magazine, mattress, mummy, nadir, sherbet, sofa,* and *sugar.*

And consider Islam's contributions in architecture. I remember visiting the Taj Mahal in Agra, India. It is a mausoleum—not exactly a tomb, but more of a monument to Mumtaz Mahal, the favorite wife of Emperor Shah Jahan, and completed in 1648. One of the eight wonders of the world, the Taj Mahal exemplifies the best of Islamic architecture. The building is phenomenally impressive, dazzling to the eye. No one can accuse the Muslims of architectural backwardness.

Islam has given us more than just language and architecture; it has also made significant contributions to music, poetry, medicine, astronomy and mathematics. During the Middle Ages, when Western culture was often in decline, the Islamic culture was in its ascendancy.

The *Avicenna* (whose name comes from Ibn Sina, a tenth-century Persian philosopher and physician) was used as a medical textbook in European universities until the seventeenth century. Ibn Sina also correctly surmised how the geologic column was formed.[45] Much of what we know about astronomy comes from Islamic scientists, and many names of stars have Arabic roots. (Consider the word *azimuth* and the stars *Aldebaran, Altair, Betelgeuse, Deneb, Rigel,* and *Vega.*) In mathematics, the number zero came from Muslims,[46] not the Europeans, as did *algorithm,* and *algebra.*[47]

Culturally, the world has certainly benefited from Islam. Having granted that, we can also admit that the world has benefited culturally from *many* movements, religions, and philosophies. Acknowledging their cultural contributions in no way implies that their religious underpinnings must be true.

Islamic Contributions

Arabic language
Arabic Numerals
Architecture
Astronomy
Algebra

Another positive trait of Islam is likely to be overlooked by Westerners. This trait of faithful Muslims is acceptance: acceptance of Allah's will. Muslims believe in fate, which they call *kismet*. Their mindset is: What is has been ordained by Allah. Do not resist fate. Be gracious. If you are dying from cancer, do not kick and scream—accept it. Your day has come. If your business goes through some tremendous disaster, Allah willed it; he allowed it. Get over it, accept what comes, and do so with dignity. Do not complain or whine. This idea of accepting not just the good, but also the bad, is an attitude that Christians would do well to learn from their Muslim neighbors.

By now, you may be wondering whether the author is inclined to become a Muslim. No, I am not. I only think we should strive to be equitable as we consider the strengths and weaknesses of any religion or philosophy.

Incandescence Versus Reflection

When we look outside on a clear night and behold the full moon, it is bright. We can read by it. It casts a shadow. The light, however, is not coming from the moon. The moon's brilliance is only a reflection of a greater light.

In the daytime, no man in his right mind would stare at the sun, since after a few seconds he would begin to go blind. The blinding light of the sun, shining 93 million miles (150 million kilometers) from Earth, bounces off the moon, which is only 240,000 miles (400,000 kilometers) from Earth. The moon reflects but a minuscule fraction of the sun's light.

In the same way, all world religions reflect some of God's light. None is totally dark. We should not be surprised when we come across truth in Islam, or Buddhism, or Taoism, because the truth of God is reflected in many places. Further, the light has been reflected in the lives of many individuals throughout history. Yet there is a difference between direct and indirect light, incandescence and reflection. Maybe this analogy will help you when you think about Islam.

We can freely acknowledge that there is a good deal of truth in Islam. A number of its teachings are similar to biblical teachings, but this light is only *reflected*. After all, Islam was built on the foundation of Christianity and Judaism. Nevertheless, Christianity and Islam have many more differences than they do similarities.

Doctrines Common to Islam and the New Testament

One God
Word of God
Faith
Obedience
Heaven
Hell
No adultery
Angels
Demons
Jesus sent by God
Virgin birth of Jesus
Second coming of Jesus
No priesthood
Obedience to God
Resurrection
Judgment Day

Grace: The Key Difference

Before we end this chapter, I would like to touch briefly on the subject of grace. The emphasis on grace, or unmerited favor, is a trait that distinguishes Christianity from other religions. Though no literary critic, I have read through the Qur'an several times. The concept of grace, as many readers have noted, is different in Islam than in Christianity.

Do not be deflected from this point by the words at the start of every sura of the Qur'an:[48] "In the name of Allah, the Compassionate, the Merciful."[49] The Islamic scriptures do mention Allah's mercy and compassion frequently. A number of passages state that Allah forgives sin.[50] Thus it would be unfair to accuse Islam of completely lacking grace.[51] However, what does the Qur'anic text actually teach about grace? We must examine not just the rhetoric, but the actual content of the faith.

Studying the Qur'an, I see that we earn grace (see 7:43, 39:61, 40:9). We earn the favor of Allah; we earn salvation and we earn paradise.[52] Fundamentally, Islam is based on works. This is the tendency of all human religions. Man-made religions are based on merit. You earn salvation; you deserve it. This is a humanistic approach. According to the humanistic mindset, *we* are taking the initiative, *we* are trying to find our way to God—when in truth, God is finding his way to us. He is taking initiative and speaking to us. Christians understand that God did this through Jesus Christ, but that concept is alien to the thinking of other religions, including Islam. The direction of the arrow is backward. We cannot find God at our own initiative. *God* reveals himself to *us*. Christians correctly understand that we can never be good enough to deserve heaven. And when we understand grace, our lives become more gracious.

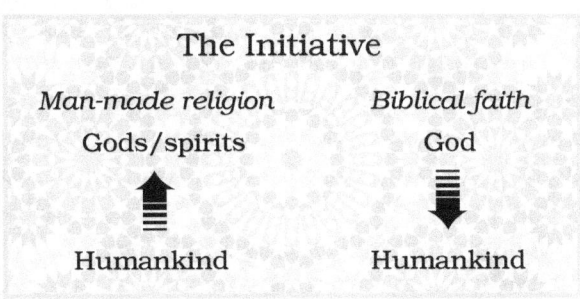

The Initiative

Man-made religion	*Biblical faith*
Gods/spirits	God
⬆	⬇
Humankind	Humankind

God's Love of Sinners

"Surely [Allah] loves not the wrongdoers," reads sura 42:30. In contrast, the Bible proclaims:

> But God proves his love for us in that while we still were sinners Christ died for us. Much more surely then, now that we have been justified by his blood, will we be saved through him from the wrath of God. For if while we were enemies, we were reconciled to God through the death of his Son, much more surely, having been reconciled, will we be saved by his life (Romans 5:8–10 NRSV).

Where is the corresponding verse in the Qur'an? It does not exist. Allah is aloof; he has no personal relationship with his creation.

While there are a few verses in the Old Testament that speak of God's enemies, these are found predominantly in the poetic sections, and it is difficult to extract a doctrine of divine hatred from them. The New Testament repeatedly emphasizes God's love for people, in countless verses. Perhaps the most famous proclamation of God's graciousness is, "For God so loved the world..." (John 3:16).

When the infinite God sent Jesus into the world, it was not because of any obligation on his part towards his finite creatures. Everything—anything—he gives to us is by his grace.

The Effect of Grace

Most human religious systems rely on offers of reward and threats of punishment in order to persuade their adherents to comply with accepted standards of behavior. In this respect, Islam is not different from the majority of world religions. Yet this stands in stark contrast with the Christian Scriptures.

When true grace is experienced by humans, it transforms our lives, affecting how we think and feel, carry ourselves, and interact with others. One area in which grace changes how we live is *motivation*. When we are motivated by grace, we tend to be happier, accomplish more, and give the credit to God, rather than accept it ourselves. As Paul wrote in 1 Corinthians 15:9–10:

> For I am the least of the apostles and do not even deserve to be called an apostle, because I persecuted the church of God. But by the grace of God I am what I am, and his grace to me was not without effect. No, I worked harder than all of them—yet not I, but the grace of God that was with me.

Yet in the Qur'an, while the grace and the mercy of Allah are often stated, they are not the motivation for right behavior. The Qur'an relies on eternal rewards and punishments as incentives, far more than does the Bible. For example, "the fire" is referred to some 140 times in the Qur'an, and "hell" ninety-eight times. Yet the New Testament, which is a significantly longer work, refers to the fire only twenty-five times, and hell thirteen times.

A memorable portion of the Qur'an declares,

> ... Surely We have prepared for the iniquitous a Fire, an enclosure of which will encompass them. And if they cry for water, they are given water like molten brass, scalding their faces. Evil the drink! And ill the resting-place! (18:29)

A second area in which the effects of grace may be clearly seen is *freedom of thought and speech*. To put it quite bluntly, in most Muslim countries, freedom of thought is discouraged and genuine public debate is prohibited. This is a fact that Muslim scholars freely concede. (They have no choice but to admit the sad reality.) Differences of viewpoint are all too easily labeled "blasphemy."[53]

To be fair, some historical perspective is needed. As Esposito and Mogahed point out, "We in the West had centuries to move from monarchies to modern democratic states, from divine-right kingdoms to modern secular nation-states, and we suffered from revolutionary and civil wars in the process. In contrast, governments in the Muslim world, created after World War II, are only decades old."[54]

Having made this qualification, we must not gloss over the fact that death is the stipulated penalty for apostasy from Islam (2:217; 4:89, 5:54, 9:11-12, 66, 73-74; 88:21).[55] The (heretical) Ismailis are among the few Muslim groups rejecting the death penalty for apostasy. At any rate, every year this sentence is carried out innumerable times around the planet.

Moreover, if the Qur'an is the *immutable* word of God, as orthodox Muslims claim it to be, then there is no way to "update" this teaching. Death is demanded for apostates.

A third effect of grace is *kindness*, and the two are often linked in the New Testament. (For a few examples, see John 1:17; 1 Corinthians 4:13, 13:4; 2 Corinthians 6:6; Galatians 5:22; Ephesians 4:32; Colossians 3:12; 1 Thessalonians 5:15; 2 Timothy 2:24; Titus 3:3ff; and 2 Peter 1:7.)

Muslims cannot fail to notice when true Christianity is put into practice. Consider the following encouraging article, which speaks to this fact:

A new study reveals why some 600 ex-Moslems decided to leave Islam to follow Jesus, even in the face of heavy persecution, sacrifice, and death threats. According to Professor Dudley Woodberry of the Fuller Theological Institute, who conducted the study, the most important reasons were as follows: "Many were attracted by the certainty of salvation in Jesus... He does not retaliate; is humble, loves the poor and outcasts; the power of His love is unique, and one can enter a relationship with Him, completely different to Islam. Christians are the only people who really work for justice for the poor and repressed; Christians' unconditional love and their peaceful and contented aura are very noticeable."[56]

These laudatory comments were made by Muslims who had converted, and perhaps their observations are somewhat overstated. After all, there are some Muslims who work for justice for the poor and the oppressed, even though the number may not be large.[57]

What is it that transforms a person, filling him or her with love, joy, peace, patience, kindness, goodness, faithfulness, gentleness, and self-control?[58] What is it that truly makes the people of God the salt of the earth and the light of the world?[59] It is the grace of God. Let not Christians take God's grace for granted, nor imagine that it is equally present in all religions. It is not.

Let us conclude with a memorable vignette that well encapsulates this point:

> During a British conference on comparative religion, experts from around the world debated what, if any, belief was unique to the Christian faith. They began eliminating the possibilities: Incarnation? Other religions have different versions of gods appearing in human form. Resurrection? Again, other religions have accounts of return from death.
>
> The debate went on for some time until C. S. Lewis[60] wandered into the room. "What's the rumpus about?" he asked, and heard in reply that his colleagues were discussing Christianity's unique contribution among world religions. Lewis responded, "Oh, that's easy. It's grace." After some discussion, the conferees had to agree. The notion of God's love coming to us free of charge, no strings attached, seems to go against every instinct of humanity. The Buddhist eight-fold path, the Hindu doctrine of karma, the Jewish covenant, the Muslim code of law—each of these offers a way to earn approval. Only Christianity dares to make God's love unconditional.[61]

JESUS AND ISLAM

3

Al-Qur'an:
The Bible of the Muslims

*A Book which We have revealed to you, in order
that you might lead mankind out of the depths
of darkness into light...*

—Al-Qur'an 14:1

Since my first days of acquaintance with Islam, I have continued to peruse the Qur'an. On my first reading, everything was new, albeit familiar, owing to heavy borrowing from the Old and New Testaments—and I made many mental and paper notes. I especially noticed divergence from the (much older) biblical text. On my second reading through, I tried harder to make sense of the incongruities in the Muslim scriptures. I also browsed alternate translations, and soon realized, from perusing the footnotes, that Muslims were well aware of the "problem passages" of their holy book. Some even tried to tone down the translation of the offensive sections. Twenty years later, during my third reading, I took an entirely different approach. I think this is because every year I have tried to become a better Bible student, paying attention to context and resisting the temptation to make a passage say what I *want* it to mean, as opposed to what it actually says. This methodology has affected how I read the Qur'an, and so it should.

I see now that all passages have historical contexts, even if the scholars cannot always agree on what they are. Some passages in the Qur'an have been pressed into service to say what they simply don't say—not only by Christians on a mission to find flaws, but also by Muslims eager to justify their own (often extreme) interpretations.

Just as most Christians are (shockingly, I think) unfamiliar with the Bible, so most Muslims are quite unfamiliar with the Qur'an. Yes, some passages are familiar to most adherents, but few have taken the time to read their sacred tome carefully. Even fewer have completed even a single reading of the entire book!

I was once on a flight from Bolivia to Chile, when a man seated across the aisle asked, "Can I see your book?"

"Sure—here it is." I handed him the handsome green volume with Arabic calligraphy on the front cover. "Are you interested in the Qur'an?"

He replied, "Well, I should be, since I'm a Muslim, but to be honest, I have never read it." (This sounds a lot like the answer you get from most "Christians," who sheepishly admit that they are not very good students of the Bible. The religions and characters vary, but the explanations are the same!)

I introduced myself. "I'm Douglas. I'm a Christian teacher."

"Ahmed," he responded, extending his hand. I then told him about my own study of the various world religions, how I had visited many mosques, and would soon be debating an eminent imam. I promised him a copy of the debate as soon as it was ready. "I guess I should be the one reading the Qur'an, not you," he said. "I'm really happy we met." Ahmed was intrigued, to say the least!

Lest I be guilty of implying that no Muslims ever read *Al-Kitab* (one of many names for the Qur'an), I should concede that there are some (like Moustafa in chapter 1) who know their scriptures well and insist on accuracy. After a talk I gave in 2008 at the University of Georgia on "Jesus and Jihad," many visitors—Christians and Muslims alike—engaged in lively discussions. Everyone was speaking and listening, hearing those on the other side, explaining and defending his or her position—it was quite an evening!

Two Muslims from the Middle East walked over to me, disturbed because they thought that in my presentation I had gotten one of the facts wrong about how the Qur'an came together. (Yes, I had oversimplified, although at the end it turned out to be a minor point.) They expected—and rightly so—accuracy from anyone teaching about such important matters. For a public speaker, feedback like this is golden. If nothing else, it helps us to make the next presentation better than the last. Yet Muslims like these, educated in their own scriptures and history, are the exception, not the rule.

Terminology

In the last chapter, we looked at the history of Islam, its growth and development, and its basic teachings, commonly called the Five Pillars. As we delve into the holy book of the Muslims, the Qur'an, let us begin with terminology, so that we are all on the same page. People often use the wrong words when talking about the Muslim faith. Sometimes I hear them getting it backwards, mistakenly calling the followers of Muhammad "Islams," and saying that Muhammad founded "Muslim." This does not work! Let's use the right terms; this also shows respect.

The book of the Muslims is the *Qur'an*, sometimes spelled "Koran" in English. The traditional spelling, however, is "Qur'an." The name of the religion is *Islam*. A follower of Muhammad is a *Muslim*, sometimes called a *Muhammadan* (or *Mohammedan*). Bringing Islam to the world by political and military needs (as necessary), as some of the radical groups intend to do, is known as *Islamism*. The Muslim legal system, which is in place in some communities and nations, is called *shari'a law.* One more term to know, particularly if you study the history of Islam, is the word *infidel.* That term is used both ways: Muslims sometimes refer to those who do not believe in Allah and his prophet Muhammad as infidels; at the same time, Christians sometimes call Muslims infidels, because they do not believe in Jesus Christ.[62]

Terminology

Qur'an, Koran	The Recitation
Sura and aya	Chapter and verse
Imam	Islamic teacher
Mullah	An Islamic cleric or learned man
Hafiz	One who has memorized the Qur'an
Hadith	Traditions
Islam	The religion
Muslim, Moslem	The follower
Shahid	A martyr for Allah
"Infidel"	The insult (used by both sides)
Tahrif	The charge that Jews or Christians have corrupted the biblical text.
Islamism	The campaign to convert the world
Shari'a law	Theological basis for Muslim law
Fatwa	A legal ruling by a Muslim scholar
Murtid	One who has apostatized from Islam

You will collect a few more useful terms throughout this book, but these are the most important. And now, having established our terminology, let us take a look at the Qur'an and its teachings. We will divide our examination into twelve parts.

1. The Qur'an: Basic Facts

The Qur'an itself was based on revelations allegedly from the archangel Gabriel to Muhammad. During the "night of destiny," divine words were dictated, and Muhammad wrote them down.[63] They did not come all at once. "Surely We have revealed the Qur'an to thee, in portions" (76:23).

Originally memorized, the rhymed Arabic prose of the Qur'an was eventually written down on whatever material was available—for example, pieces of palm leaf, scraps of leather, stones, even camel shoulder bones—and eventually these various scraps were collected.

The compilation of these writings took place shortly after the lifetime of Muhammad, in the mid-600s. The writings were arranged roughly from longest to shortest, and each chapter is called a "sura." The exception to the pattern is the short sura 1, which serves as the introduction to the entire Qur'an. Suras 2 through 114 follow. The order is not chronological, and some suras are composite documents. There were several versions of the Qur'an before Uthman (Caliph 580–656) standardized the text.

The Qur'an is about eighty percent the length of the New Testament. Many years ago, when I first began to explore the Muslim scriptures, I was surprised (and encouraged) by how short it is, and decided to dive in. I knew I would read the Bible many times through as a Christian, and so I thought, "Why not read the Qur'an?" At least then I would know what it says. After I finished it the first time, I decided to read it again, just in case I had missed something. Besides, I knew this would help me understand and connect with Muslims even more. Given its manageable length, I think it is a good idea for the serious Christian to become familiar with this document. Even if you don't read it completely, at least you can become familiar with the content.

Often Muslims say that the Qur'an is written in pure Arabic, and should therefore only be read in the original.[64] After all, it is the language of heaven, spoken by Allah and the holy angels. It is even affirmed that the original Qur'an is a perfect copy of the heavenly Qur'an.[65] Many Muslim scholars go so far as to insist that all translations of the Qur'an are

Chronology

570 AD	Birth of Muhammad[66]
596	Marriage to Khadijah (d. 619)
610	Gabriel speaks to Muhammad
612	First mosque built in India
615	Islam comes to Abyssinia (Africa)
622	The Hijrah (Mecca to Medina)
630	Mecca taken
632	Final suras dictated; death of Muhammad; rise of Caliphate
650	Qur'an compiled under Uthman (son-in-law of Muhammad)
660+	All of Arabia Muslim
711	Islam dominant in southern Spain
732	Battle of Tours
750	Umayyad Dynasty (based in Damascus) ends; 'Abassid Dynasty begins (Baghdad)
1100+	Islam reaches Indonesia
1258	Mongol invasion; Baghdad sacked
1380+	Islam reaches the Philippines
1453	Fall of Constantinople to Ottomans
1492	Moors driven out of Spain
1648	Taj Mahal completed under Moguls
1798	Napoleon invades Egypt
1915	Muslim wives permitted to initiate divorce
1917	Ottoman Law of Family Rights passed
1918	Dissolution of Ottoman Empire
2001	Attacks on New York and Washington, D.C.

interpretations, and hence lack the authority of the original.

There are a few problems with this claim. To begin with, as we will see, the claim that the Qur'an is a perfect copy is simply false, because there is more than one version of the book, even today. Some suras are now missing from the text.

For example, the *Surat al-Hafd* says: "You (alone) we worship, and to You (alone) we pray and lie prostrate, and to You (alone) we proceed and have descendants. We fear Your torture and hope for Your mercy. Truly Your torture will overtake the infidels." And the *Surat al-Khal'* reads: "O Allah, You (alone) we ask for help and forgiveness. We speak appreciatively of Your goodness. Never do we disbelieve You. We repudiate and disbelieve anyone who follows immorality."[67]

Next, we must ask whether Arabic is really "the language of heaven." Would it not be more fair to say that Allah knows all languages?

Another difficulty is that the Qur'an is not written in just one language. It *is* written primarily in Arabic, but many words from other languages slipped in, including Persian, Ethiopic, Akkadian, Syriac, Greek, Hebrew, and Egyptian. So much for the claim that the Qur'an is written in *pure* Arabic.

A final problem is that only twenty percent of Muslims speak Arabic as a first language. Add to this low literacy rates in the Muslim world and we see that only the minority can read their scriptures in the original tongue. Muslims will often say, "You can never fully understand the Qur'an unless you read it in Arabic." But once again, most Muslims do not read Arabic. They read Farsi, Indonesian, Turkish or some other language, but not the original tongue. The truth is, we can understand the Qur'an in translation—at least the words, if not always the meaning—just as we can understand the Bible by reading it in translation.

As English readers, we must be careful in selecting which version of the Qur'an to read, just as we are when we select an English Bible. Some versions are only paraphrases. The difficult passages have been eliminated or smoothed over. Be sure you are reading a good translation.[68]

Some Muslim scholars add a caution at this point. They admit that most of the Qur'an is difficult to understand. For example, the secular Muslim Ali Dashti lamented the literary defects of the Qur'an: "Unfortunately the Qur'an was badly edited and its contents are very obtusely arranged."[69] Dashti was tortured to death by the Islamic regime in Iran in 1982. Anyone reading the Qur'an will soon admit that the task is not easy going, as I myself have experienced. This also explains why the Qur'anic experts often disagree over matters of interpretation.

2. Islam and Morality

Generally speaking, the moral standards of Islam and the Qur'an are *lower* than those of the New Testament but *higher* than those of most who claim to be Christians. (Note: I am using the word *Christian* in its broadest possible sense.) Let us consider just a few moral areas.

Adultery

The Qur'an requires severe corporal punishment for adultery. "The woman and the man guilty of illegal sexual intercourse—flog each of them with a hundred stripes. Let not pity withhold you in their case, in a punishment prescribed by Allah, if you believe in Allah and the Last Day. And let a party of the believers witness their punishment" (24:2). In *shari'a* law, it is claimed that this refers to unmarried people; married offenders are stoned to death, in accordance with the teaching of the Hadith.[70]

Below the New Testament standard: Jesus taught that even lust is a sin (Matthew 5:28). On the other hand, he also urged grace for offenders, as we see in the account of the woman caught in adultery (John 7:53–8:11).[71]

Above the common Christian standard: In the Christian West, political freedoms include the right to produce, publish, and watch pornography. Premarital sex and homosexuality are defended, and even among the evangelical churches, extramarital sex is often condoned, sometimes even when committed by church leaders.

Social Concern

Though it hardly stands in the fierce prophetic tradition of the Old Testament, the Qur'an, like the Hebrew and Christian Scriptures, commends care for the poor. As we read in 90:12–18: "And what will make thee comprehend what the uphill road is? (It is) to free a slave, or to feed in a day of hunger an orphan nearly related, or the poor man lying in the dust. Then he is of those who believe and exhort one another to patience, and exhort one another to mercy. These are the people of the right hand."

Below the New Testament standard: Although this sura 90 is certainly similar to Jesus' teaching in Matthew 25:31–46, the emphasis on care for the needy in the Qur'an as a whole is not as strong as it is in the New Testament. Moreover, notice that Christianity rises above culture more than Islam. Followers of Christ are more likely than Muslims to adopt an orphan entirely unrelated to them.

Above the common Christian standard: The affluent Christian West gives a pittance of its wealth to the needy. A sad but well-known fact is that the average citizen of the United States spends more annually on dog food than it gives to the poor. Islam requires Muslims to give one-fortieth of their income to the needy. This is more than most Christians give.

Aggression

Islam allows warfare, though not unjustified aggression. "And fight in the way of Allah against those who fight against you, but be not aggressive. Surely Allah loves not the aggressors" (2:190). To put it another way, don't start a fight, but if someone is opposing Allah, you are entitled to engage in warfare.

Below the New Testament standard: Jesus forbade killing one's enemies (Matthew 5:20-21, 38ff).

Above the common Christian standard: Most modern Christians see little problem in ignoring Jesus' teaching on this subject, especially if required by their governments to kill. (We will discuss this problem in chapter 5.)

Pure Speech

No obscenities or fighting were allowed during the *hajj*, or pilgrimage (2:197), thus indicating that obscenity was in fact condoned at other times.

Below the New Testament standard: Jesus and the inspired writers of the New Testament *never* permit swearing or obscenity (Matthew 5:33ff; 12:34; Ephesians 4:29; 5:4; James 1:26, etc).

Above the common Christian standard: The speech of most who claim to be Christian today is no different than the speech of non-believers. To most, it seems all sense of holiness has been lost.

Alcohol and Gambling

An earlier passage of the Qur'an, 2:219, does not prohibit alcohol and gambling, it only warns of the dangers: "They ask thee about intoxicants and games of chance. Say: In both of them is a great sin and (some) advantage for men, and their sin outweighs their advantage..." In other words, though the bad outweighs the good, these activities are not to be forbidden. A later passage, 5:90, is stronger in its condemnation: "O you who believe, intoxicants and games of chance... are only an uncleanness, the devil's work; so shun it that you may succeed." Strict Muslims today touch no alcohol.

Equal to the New Testament standard: Though the Bible does not speak highly of alcohol or gambling (see Proverbs 23:29ff; Luke 21:34; Romans 13:13), nowhere is it specifically forbidden. In this respect the Qur'an and the Bible appear to be on the same level.

Above the common Christian standard: Whereas most Muslims avoid alcohol, the overwhelming majority of Christians drink it, and often to excess.

Modest Dress

Muslim modesty is well-known. Consider the following passage: "Say to the believing men that they lower their gaze and restrain their sexual passions. That is purer for them. Surely Allah is Aware of what they do. And say to the believing women they lower their gaze and restrain their sexual passions and do not display their adornment except what appears thereof. And let them wear their head-coverings over their bosoms. And should not display their adornment except to their husbands or their fathers, or the fathers of their husbands, or their sons, or the sons of their husbands, or their brothers, or their brothers' sons, or their sisters' sons, or their women, or those whom their right hands possess, or guileless male servants, or the children who know not a woman's nakedness..." (24:30–31).

Beyond the New Testament standard: Though the New Testament insists on modesty, it says nothing about which parts of the body must be covered, except for the female head covering in 1 Corinthians 11—which most Christians interpret as a cultural requirement. (There are, however, several Old Testament passages, such as Ezekiel 16 and 23, which point the people of God to sexual propriety.) To modern Christians, the Qur'an feels prudish.

Above the common Christian standard: Most Western Christians give little thought to modesty, despite the New Testament scriptures urging it (1 Timothy 2:9–10; 1 Peter 3:3–4).

Muslims also tend to be less focused on women's physical appearance. As a result, studies have shown that there are few eating disorders (anorexia, bulimia) compared to the West. There is something to be said for the veil and the burqa! This is not to say that Muslims don't *want* to see what is under a woman's clothes. Leading a large tour group to Egypt, I spoke to my Muslim hosts about Christian habits. I explained that some of the tour members drank wine, though not to excess. This conformed with their stereotypes of the West. But they couldn't understand why I cancelled the belly dancer! A frank discussion about modesty ensued, and I believe they were able to see their inconsistency in covering up a woman during the day, but "undressing" her in the evening. (In place of the belly dancer, we settled on a dervish, who was as modest in his dress as he was impressive in his gyrations.)

Summary

While the Qur'an does not match the high standard of the New Testament, it nonetheless demands a higher standard than that to which most churchgoers adhere. For example, Islam prohibits abortion after the fortieth day; see 17:31 and also 81:8–9, which forbids female infanticide (burying unwanted daughters alive). Although Christians do not normally commit infanticide, many have a casual attitude towards abortion.

It should hardly surprise us that many Muslims worldwide equate Christianity with decadence. For sadly, in their eyes, the decadent West is the Christian West.[72]

3. Islam and Degrees of Sin

The Qur'an promotes the idea of salvation by works—that is, that certain sins may be forgiven if good deeds outweigh evil ones.

Sura 11:114 reads, "Surely good deeds take away evil deeds." I believe this sort of sentiment is a natural, human way of thinking—even for Christians, who believe in salvation by grace. When I do wrong, I want to make it up somehow. If you find me behaving politely to others, putting them before myself, it *may* be because I want to follow the teachings of Jesus Christ and respect my fellow man. But it may also be because earlier today I was rude to someone and I feel bad about it. Do you relate? We do a bad thing, our conscience bothers us a little bit, and then we do a good thing to try to atone. When we think this way, we are adhering to an idea similar to that promoted by the Qur'an: "Surely good deeds take away evil deeds."

In the Qur'an, we find three levels of sin. First, there are the big sins, the *kabira*, like murder, adultery, drunkenness, disobeying your parents, failing to observe Ramadan (the month of fasting), neglecting Friday prayers, gambling, dancing, shaving your beard, charging interest, and forgetting the Qur'an after you read it. If you commit one of these sins, you can be forgiven only if you repent.

Then there are little sins, the *saghira*. These are offenses like deceit, anger, or lust. Forgiveness will certainly be given as long as the greater sins are avoided and good deeds are performed.[73] So a good deed would wipe out the little sins. Whereas the big sins, the *kabira*, are not wiped out unless you repent, the *saghira* are not that significant.

But there is a third category, the most serious sin, called *shirk*. Shirk means association; that is, associating other gods with Allah. These partner gods might be daughters or sons, as many in ancient times imagined that the gods procreated. Sura 112 deals exclusively with this matter:

In the name of Allah, the Beneficent, the Merciful.
Say: He, Allah, is One.
Allah is He on Whom all depend.
He begets not, nor is he begotten;
And none is like Him.

Or consider 4:48:

Surely Allah forgives not that a partner should be set up with Him, and forgives all besides that to whom He pleases. And whoever sets up a partner with Allah, he devises indeed a great sin.

In effect, if you say, "Let's worship Allah and his wife," then you are saying that there is more than one god. If you say,

"Jesus is the son of God; in fact, Jesus was God in the flesh," you are also guilty of shirk. Many, many passages warn against associating other gods with Allah.[74] The Qur'an teaches that it is impossible to be forgiven while committing shirk.

Three Levels of Sin

The Big Sins: *Kabira*
• Examples: Murder, adultery, drunkenness, disobedience to parents, failing to observe Ramadan, neglecting Friday prayers, gambling, dancing, shaving the beard, charging interest, forgetting Qur'an after reading it
• Forgiven only if you repent

The Little Sins: *Saghira*
• Examples: Deceit, anger, lust
• Forgiven if you avoid greater sins and perform good deeds

The Unforgivable Sin: *Shirk*
• Definition: Associating other gods with Allah
• Example: Making Jesus God
• Cannot be forgiven

4. The Judgment

All will be resurrected (4:87). "Allah, there is no god but He—He will certainly gather you together on the Resurrection day, there is no doubt about it..." (6:36). After the resurrection is the last judgment. The Qur'an repeatedly speaks of but two eternal destinies: the Fire and the Garden. Unbelievers, including idolaters and hypocrites, will be thrown into the fire.

Has there come to thee the news of the Overwhelming Event? Faces on that day will be downcast, Laboring, toiling, entering burning Fire, made to drink from a boiling spring. They will have no food but of thorns, neither nourishing nor satisfying hunger (88:1–7).

Faithful Muslims, on the other hand, will enjoy the Garden: "Faces on that day will be happy—glad for their striving—in a lofty Garden" (88:8–10). The strictest versions of Islam allow only practicing Muslims into paradise.

And whoever seeks a religion other than Islam, it will not be accepted from him, and in the Hereafter he will be one of the losers (3:84).

5. Women

Many suras mention men and women together, as equal partners in spiritual life. Other passages make the Christian reader cringe. Sura 4, for example, reads:

Men have authority over women because God has made the one superior to the other, and because they spend their wealth to maintain them. Good women are obedient. They guard their unseen parts because God has guarded them. As for those from whom you fear disobedience, admonish them and forsake them in beds apart, and beat them... (4:34).

Not surprisingly, this passage has been toned down in some versions of the Qur'an. I have studied the Qur'an in several different English translations, and two of them render the passage as I have quoted it here. Two others totally reword it, probably in an effort to appear less sexist or more sophisticated.[75]

Sura 4:3 also says, "Marry women of your choice, two, three, or four."[76] The Qur'an teaches that men can marry up to four women. But how many wives did Muhammad have? Some researchers find that he had sixteen legal wives, not to mention the two slaves whom he slept with, and four other women who were neither his slaves nor his wives—for a total of twenty-two women! His third wife, whom he took from his son-in-law, was only eight or nine years old at the time. So Muhammad had something of a "harem." In my own reading of the Qur'an, I found the names of nine of his wives. One of them was Jewish, another a nominal Ethiopian Christian.

It is noteworthy that, while Muhammad had perhaps twenty-two women, the Qur'an limits the number of wives for all other Muslim males to four. On the other hand, in defense of Muhammad, it seems he lived faithfully with his first wife, Khadijah, until her death. Only afterwards did Muhammad take other wives.

In fact, in the Shia version of Islam, for a fee, one may even become "married"—for the sake of carnal pleasure. After an hour or two (presumably the fee rises depending on the length of the "marriage") the man receives a legal "divorce." We would call this racket, sanctified though it may be, *prostitution*.[77]

Yet it must also be noted—partially balancing out the previous criticisms—that modern Muslim women often feel that Western culture (with its indecent dress, promiscuous behavior, and pornography), is far more degrading to women than Muslim culture. And on this score, it is hard to disagree.

6. Paradise

When Muslims use the word *paradise*, they do not employ it in the early Christian sense of the term, the place where the righteous dead await the Day of Judgment. Paradise for the Muslim means heaven, a garden of refreshment into which Allah brings his true servants. In sura 37:40–49 we read:

> The true servants of Allah will be well provided for, feasting on fruit and honored in the gardens of delight. Reclining face to face upon soft couches, they shall be served with a goblet filled at a gushing fountain, white, and delicious to those who drink it. They shall sit with bashful, dark-eyed virgins, as chaste as the sheltered eggs of ostriches.

This passage presents paradise as an oasis in the desert. Given the culture of the times, this is an understandable image.

You will have noticed that the "true servants of Allah" appear to be men. In another passage, paradise is called "a band of brothers." Other passages, such as 40:40 and 4:124, mention women in paradise, but they are often serving the men, rather than enjoying it themselves. I am not referring to Muslim writings outside the Qur'an, which are more voluminous and broad than the Qur'an. I am only referring to the Qur'an itself.

The Qur'an depicts paradise as a place where men recline on couches (as people often ate in the ancient world), drinking and being attended by *houris*, the "bashful, dark-eyed virgins." These virgins are found in 44:54; 52:20; 56:36-38; and much of sura 55. Consider, for example 52:20 (the three versions below are the three authorized English translations of the Qur'an):

Yusufali: They will recline (with ease) on Thrones (of dignity) arranged in ranks; and We shall join them to Companions, with beautiful big and lustrous eyes.

Pickthal: Reclining on ranged couches. And we wed them unto fair ones with wide, lovely eyes.

Shakir: Reclining on thrones set in lines, and We will unite them to large-eyed beautiful ones.

Paradise is a place of wine, women, and song. Is it not odd that the things that are forbidden in this life are the reward in the next life?[78]

7. Errors

If you are familiar with the Old and New Testament, you will be struck not just by how many times the Qur'an borrows from the Bible, but also by how often it incorrectly describes some biblical event—sometimes deliberately changing the story. Historical errors are rampant. Of course the Muslim commentators try to harmonize the differences, but this does not always work. They normally attribute error to the Bible, claiming that the original was correct, but mistakes crept in through the process of scribal transmission.

Muhammad's knowledge of the Scriptures was mediated through the Jews and Christians with whom he interacted. Because their beliefs and practices were not always biblical, Muhammad ended up absorbing many of their errant notions. And thus many things he attributes to Christianity and the Christian Bible are inaccurate.

In a sense, he understood seventh-century Christianity all too well. After all, how much did Christian followers—and even leaders—believe in, or even know about, the Bible at this time? How many innovations had crept into the faith since apostolic times? This is the period many refer to as the Dark Ages—and they were dark in more ways than one. Muhammad's writings probably reflected the common beliefs and spirituality of his day, not only in polytheistic Arabia but also in the Christian world.

To give a couple of examples, we read in the Qur'an about Jesus' childhood miracles (3:48; 5:110). Jesus even begins speaking from the cradle (3:45; 5:110; 19:30)![79] And yet Jesus did not perform childhood miracles, as far as we know. Only in the second century did some Christians write fanciful stories about the pranks and wonders the boy Jesus supposedly performed. These apocrypha are well known.

For example, one tale recounts the boy Jesus making some pigeons out of clay. He did this on the Sabbath, thus breaking some Sabbath law. To avoid getting in trouble, he turned the clay birds into real pigeons and they flew away.[80] Another story claims that when Jesus was playing, things got a bit rough, and a boy fell off the balcony and died. How did young Jesus get around it? He raised him from the dead.[81] And there are other apocryphal miracles besides these two.

These stories result from natural human curiosity. In the second century, many Christians began to wonder what Jesus was like as a boy, and so people devised all kinds of stories. Similarly, the Buddha did not perform any miracles, but sometime after his death, his followers created the necessary tales. You can read about the miracles Buddha supposedly performed as a little boy in the *Jataka Tales*. These inflated legends came into being, somewhat predictably, just like the childhood miracles of Jesus, yet they are not true at all.

Many Catholic Christians of the seventh century believed these tales about Jesus' boyhood. Presumably that is where Muhammad heard them, and thus these and other historically inaccurate tales found their way into the Qur'an.

Other errors are simply based on ignorance, or perhaps a too-hasty reading of the Bible. For example, in sura 19, Mary the mother of Jesus (ayat 16ff) is mistaken as Miriam, sister of Aaron (aya 28). In the Arabic, after all, both have the same name (Miriam). Efforts to cover over this embarrassing error do not convince. For example, Muslim apologists insist Mary was of the tribe of Levi only by ignoring the clear genealogical evidence of Matthew 1. Besides, Numbers 36:6 seems to discourage intertribal marriages.

The Qur'an has difficulty with the intertwined concepts of the Trinity and of Jesus as God's son. "Unbelievers are those that say: 'God is one of three.' There is but one God" (5:73). This is a clear allusion to the Christians, who believe in the triune nature of God: Father, Son, and Spirit. But in Muhammad's day, what *was* this "trinity"? The Qur'an describes the Trinity as Allah, Isa, and Maryam (God, Jesus, and Mary). And in truth, in Catholic Arabia, Mary *was* worshiped, along with Jesus and the saints and God. So the wrong concept of the Trinity, in this case, came from the church itself.

To illustrate some of the Qur'an's many historical problems, in sura 37, who is offered, Ishmael or Isaac? In Genesis 22, Abraham is willing to sacrifice his son, his only son whom he loves, Isaac. But, in Muslim tradition, it is Ishmael (Isaac's older half-brother) that he is sacrificing. Early Muslims vacillated as to which of Abraham's sons was to be offered, but by the tenth century, Muslims decided on Ishmael. Sura 37 never says Ishmael was sacrificed, and in fact the mention of Isaac soon after the incident implied that he, the younger son, was the intended victim.[82]

In Genesis we read that Abraham's father was Terah, while in the Qur'an, it appears to be a different man, Azar.[83] In the Qur'an, Abraham does not settle in Hebron as Genesis tells us; instead, he goes to Mecca, which is far from Hebron.

The Qur'an also says that Abraham rebuilt the Kaaba, the sacred black rock (found in Mecca), and yet there is no biblical record of Abraham doing this.

The Qur'an also states Abraham was thrown into the fire by Nimrod. This is not possible for two reasons. First, it was Daniel's friends, Shadrach, Meshach, and Abednego, who were thrown into the fire—not Abraham (Daniel 3). As for Nimrod, he lived long before the time of Abraham (Genesis 10:8–9). So the story as the Qur'an tells it is simply impossible. Also, the Qur'an disagrees with Genesis about the number of sons and wives Abraham had.

Genesis is based on ancient records. Abraham lived around 2000 BC. Even the final form of Genesis dates to many centuries before Christ. The Qur'an was written 1200 to 1500 *years* after those early records—another possible reason why the facts have gotten confused.

The Qur'an is not only incorrect about the events of Abraham's life. It commits many additional errors. In Genesis, we read about both the tree of the knowledge of good and evil, and the tree of life. Yet sura 20, referring to the Garden of Eden, mentions only one tree in the garden; the two trees are combined into one, the tree of knowledge *and* life. Yet in Genesis, there was no prohibition against eating the fruit from the tree of life, only from eating the fruit of the tree of knowledge of good and evil. As with many of other inaccuracies in the Qur'an, the reference is not totally wrong. In a sense, it does mention both trees, but mingles the details.

The Qur'an commits several more errors about stories from the book of Genesis. In sura 11, we read of Noah's fourth son, who drowned in the Flood. Yet according to the Bible, Noah had only three sons: Ham, Shem, and Japheth. We read in sura 15 that clay stones fell upon and destroyed Sodom and Gomorrah, whereas the biblical record talks about fire and brimstone (sulfur).[84]

In sura 20:70, Pharaoh's magicians repented, yet we do not read about their repentance in the original source (Exodus), do we? In sura 2, the stories found in Judges 7 and 1 Samuel 17 are conflated. Judges 7 tells the story of Gideon, the judge who rallied a small band of men to defeat the Midianites. 1 Samuel 17, the events of which take place centuries later, recounts the story of David and Goliath. And yet the Qur'an has combined these two stories into a single battle scene, despite the interval of centuries. It is presented as one commingled account, as though both events took place at the same time.

Some Qur'anic Errors

Ishmael replaces Isaac—37:102 (traditional view)

Two trees in Eden become one tree—20:120

Noah's fourth son drowns—11:43

Clay stones fall on Sodom and Gomorrah—15:74

Pharaoh's magicians repent—20:70

Judges 7 and 1 Samuel 17 conflated—2:249

Zechariah silent for three days (see Luke 1:20!)—3:40

Jesus' childhood miracles—3:48, 5:110, 19:30

Another problem is found in sura 18:86, where we read about a traveler, probably Abraham.[85] He was journeying west, "till, when he reached the setting place of the sun, he found it setting in a muddy spring."

"Muddy spring" could also be translated "a black sea." The traveler found the setting place of the sun—in a muddy spring. All people—Christians and Muslims, weathermen and scientists—talk about sunset, a common, though scientifically inaccurate, word. We use the word "sunset" because it is just too awkward to scientifically describe the process of nightfall. The Bible too uses the popular terminology to describe sunrise and sunset; however, it does not say that every night the sun is extinguished in some body of water. So we see that the description in the Qur'an, even if you allow for the culture of the day, still ends up positing ludicrous error.

And this is just one example of amusing scientific inaccuracy. In suras 34 and 52, we read about a piece of the sky falling to the earth. One of the more humorous "problem passages" is 27:18, where we seem to encounter talking ants! These are a few of the Qur'anic difficulties.[86] Efforts to explain them away fall short.

8. The Famous "Satanic Verses"

In 1988, Ahmed Salman Rushdie, a British Indian writer who resides in the Atlanta area, authored a controversial book, *The Satanic Verses*.[87] It had hardly been published when a *fatwa*, or Islamic legal ruling, was issued against him by Iran's Ayatollah Khomeini, calling for his assassination. His publisher survived being shot in the back; his translators were also attacked, one fatally. Rushdie was forced to go into hiding for many years; only recently was the death decree lifted. Over the years, many persons have been subject to fatwas, merely for publishing anything "critical" of Islam, the Qur'an, or the Prophet.

What did Rushdie write that was worthy of death? The

book was certain to draw fire from Muslims, for many reasons. One is that names of the prostitutes in a brothel in the novel are the names of Muhammad's wives! This is just one of many elements in *The Satanic Verses* that are insensitive to Muslims. The initial, and perhaps greatest, offense came from the title itself. The title refers to a revelation given to Muhammad, but then retracted once it was realized that he had been tricked by Satan. But in Arabic, the word "verses" in the title was rendered *ayat*, a word referring to Qur'anic verses. Thus it sounded as if Rushdie was saying that the Qur'an itself was Satanic. By the way, Rushdie was knighted by the Queen in 2007.

What are the Satanic verses? The Qur'an names Allah's daughters, who were worshiped in Mecca in pre-Islamic times. It seems that in the passage in question, which begins at sura 53, verse 19, Muhammad (presumably in a moment of weakness) allowed worship to Allah's daughters, Al-Lat, Al-Uzza, and Manat, whose intercession was considered efficacious:

> Have you thought of Allāt and al-'Uzzā and Manāt, the third, the other? *These are the exalted intermediaries [cranes] whose intercession is to be hoped for...*

The italicized sentence was retracted. The text now reads:

> Have you thought of Allāt and al-'Uzzā and Manāt, the third, the other? For you males and for Him females? That would be unfair sharing. They are but names which you have named, you and your fathers; Allah revealed no authority for them; they [the worshippers of idols] follow only opinion and their soul's fancies, though from their Lord there has come to them guidance.

Of course this is problematic, since Muslims staunchly insist that their scriptures have never been altered in any way. Rushdie and others know, from reputable Muslim accounts of at-Tabari and Ibn Sa'd, what happened historically. And yet Muslims—including Muslim scholarship—seem to be in denial about the implications.

> In the name of Allah, the Beneficent, the Merciful.
> Praise be to Allah, the Lord of the worlds.
> The Compassionate, the Merciful!
> Master of the day of Judgment.
> Thee do we worship and to Thee do we cry for help.
> Guide us on the straight path,
> The path of those upon whom Thou hast been gracious—
> With whom Thou art not angry, and who go not astray.
>
> —Qur'an 1[88]

9. Incorruptible Qur'an Versus Corrupted Bible?

It is normally held by Muslims that the Qur'an is pure (perfectly true in every part and perfectly preserved through the centuries), whereas the Bible is corrupt (originally true but gradually corrupted). Several facts must be processed as we process this claim.

At the time of Islam's founding, the Jewish and Christian faiths were already well-established—Judaism for some two thousand years, Christianity for six hundred. Once again, Muhammad knew most of the biblical stories of the Old and New Testaments, and makes references and allusions to the Bible throughout the Qur'an, as well as to the Apocrypha.[89]

Muslims, Jews, and Christians share many common teachings. The Qur'an teaches the unity of God, the reality of angels, Satan, judgment, and so forth—and yet the differences are significant.

The Qur'an actually *upholds* the inspiration of the Bible. In sura 5, Christians are told to follow the word of God in the gospel. In sura 5:47, the Qur'an says that the people of the gospel should follow the gospel:

Common Teachings

Topic	The Qur'an	The Bible
God is one	30:42; 34:22	Deuteronomy 6:4; Ephesians 4:6
God is fair	26:209; 50:29	Genesis 18:25; Deuteronomy 32:4
God forgives sin	22:60; 4:100	Mark 2:10; Ephesians 1:7
God speaks in his Word	14:1	Psalm 19; 119
The devil is real	15:30ff.	1 Peter 5:8; 2 Cor. 11:14
Angels are real	13:11	Hebrews 1:14; 1 Peter 3:22
Resist the world	57:20	James 4:4; 1 John 2:15–17
Strive for moderation	25:67	Proverbs 30:8
Lying is a sin	16:105	Ephesians 4:25; Rev. 1:8
Adultery is a sin	24:2	Exodus 20:14; Heb. 13:4
Fornication is a sin	17:32	Galatians 5:19
Homosexuality is a sin	7:81; 27:54–55	Romans 1:26–27; 1 Corinthians 6:9
The Judgment Day	36:51; 88:2ff.	2 Peter 3:7; Romans 14:12
Heaven	37:40-49	Colossians 1:5; 2 Tim. 4:18
Hell	18:2	Mark 9:43ff; 2 Thess. 1:8-9
Care for the poor	90:12–18	Galatians 2:10; James 1:27
Prayer	62:9	1 Thessalonians 5:17
O.T. prophets	3:83	Num. 12:6-8; 2 Pet. 1:19–21
Gospel message is true	3:3	Eph. 1:13; 1 Thess. 2:13
Jesus born of a Virgin	19:19–21	Matthew 1:23; Luke 1:27
Jesus to come back	43:61	John 14:3; 1 Thessalonians 4:16; Hebrews 9:28

The people of the Injil [gospel][90] shall rule in accordance with Allah's revelations which are found there. Anyone who does not rule in accordance with Allah's revelations, these are the wicked.

In essence, the passage says that if you fail to do what Allah tells you to do, that is evil. It also explicitly states that people of the Injil (the gospel) shall obey Allah's revelations therein. Muhammad apparently believed it was possible—not only possible, but *required*—for Christians to obey Allah by following the Injil. Similarly, "the people of the book," as they are called, were told to follow the Old Testament teachings.

Many parts of the Qur'an, like this one, reveal friendly relations with Jews and Christians. However, other parts of the Qur'an—particularly those reflecting times of greater polarization—show tension. But the positive parts say that People of the Book must follow the Old Testament (for example, in suras 6:92, 37:117 and 40:53). Consider the following passages:

O you who believe, believe in Allah and His Messenger and the Book which He has revealed to His Messenger and the Book which He revealed before. And whoever disbelieves in Allah and his angels and His Books and His messengers and the Last Day, he indeed strays far away (4:136).

Say: We believe in Allah and that which is revealed to us, and that which was revealed to Abraham and Ishmael and Isaac and Jacob and the tribes, and that which was given to Moses and Jesus and the prophets from their Lord; we make no distinction between any of them, and to Him we submit (3:83).

Surely We revealed the Torah, having guidance and light. By it did the prophets who submitted themselves (to Allah) judge for the Jews, and the rabbis and the doctors of the law, because they were required to guard the Book of Allah, and they were witnesses thereof... And whoever judges not by what Allah has revealed, those are the disbelievers (5:44).

He has revealed to thee the Book with truth, verifying that which is before it, and He revealed the Torah and the Gospel aforetime, a guidance for the people, and He sent the Discrimination [which helps us to distinguish truth from error]. Those who disbelieve in the messages of Allah—for them is a severe chastisement. And Allah is Mighty, the Lord of retribution (3:3).

Why this discussion? Because Muslims today claim that the Qur'an has never changed, whereas the Christian Bible has been corrupted, and is now untrustworthy.[91] When a Christian tries to use the Bible to share his faith with a Muslim, the Muslim typically dismisses its authority, saying "Your Bible has been corrupted."[92] Why does he not follow the Qur'an on this point? "And dispute ye not with the people of the book but say: We believe in the revelation which has come down to us and that which came down to you" (29:46). Why the *dispute?* On what facts do Muslims base these claims of corruption? If the Bible was changed, then what documents was Muhammad referring to in the Qur'an? A good response to a Muslim who claims that the Bible has been changed is that the Qur'an denies this possibility. The words of Allah *cannot* be changed (Qur'an 6:34; 10:64; 18:27).

Consider the time sequence! Muhammad lived in the 600s, but we have *copies* of every book of the Bible from *long* before his time—230 manuscripts in all before the seventh century. Our most ancient Old Testament manuscript fragments currently go back to the seventh or sixth century BC. The Dead Sea scrolls, containing nearly every Old Testament book, including the prophecies of Christ, were written mainly in the third to first centuries BC. Copies of the New Testament books date to the second century AD. I have seen the oldest collection of the Apostle Paul's letters, and they date from the late second century—that is, in the 100s AD! I have even held in my hands the oldest extant New Testament manuscript,[93] from about 120 AD.

So if the Christians changed the manuscripts, why are the only surviving manuscripts in agreement with modern Bibles? And why do we find no examples, no copies of the corrupt manuscripts modern Muslims refer to? In fact, the charge that Christians have changed the Bible was never made by early Muslims; it came about in debate many centuries after Muhammad's time.

Timeline: Qur'an and Bible
(dates approximate)

400 BC	Old Testament completed
200 BC	Oldest surviving O. T. manuscripts[94]
100 AD	New Testament completed
650 AD	Bulk of Qur'an completed
800 AD	Final version of Qur'an

Modern Muslims say that the Qur'an has not changed, whereas the Bible has hundreds of thousands of variants. Yes, there are variants. In nearly every case, these are only trivial differences of spelling or word order. (*Jesus Christ* instead of *Christ Jesus*, accidental omissions in one manuscript of a word that appears in all the others, etc.) None of these variations affects any matter of doctrine.

It is true that the Bible has 200,000 to 300,000 variants. With approximately 31,000 verses, and five to ten variants per verse, that seems like a lot of errors! Once again, the discrepancies are minor. Besides, if *one* spelling error found its way into a family of one hundred manuscripts, it would be counted as one hundred errors. Yet the truth is, most verses in most versions read the same. The variants, relatively speaking, are few and far between.

It is noteworthy that while Christians have preserved the variants in their writings, the Muslims have tried to erase them from the record. When making copies of the Bible manuscripts, generally speaking, scribes chose to retain these textual variants.[95] If one scribe spelled a word a certain way, the next copied what he saw in front of him. It is significant to note that while Christians have preserved the variants in their writings, the Muslims tried to erase them from the record.

So is it true that the Qur'an has never changed? No, not at all. For example, in 1970 new manuscripts were discovered in Sanaa, Yemen. Workmen found ancient copies of the Qur'an, under a mosque.[96] Interestingly, the text jumped from sura 19 to sura 22. Two suras, 20 and 21, were missing. Then, from sura 26, the text jumped to sura 37! This manuscript has been dated to 705–715 AD, making it the oldest surviving Qur'an by half a century. The Qur'an evolved! It wasn't until the early ninth century that "complete" Qur'an appears in the historical record.

There were originally a number of different versions of the Qur'an—in Medina, Mecca, Basra, Damascus, and Kufa—up until the late 600s. But in order to bring uniformity to the religion—and unity, it was hoped—all the versions except for one were gathered and burned. Uthman (580–656) ordered all versions destroyed except the version from Medina (the adopted home of Muhammad after the hijrah).

What were unearthed in Yemen were pre-Uthmanic versions of the Qur'an. Therefore, we have archaeological proof that modern Muslims' claims are false: All Qur'ans in the world do not agree, nor are they all copies of the original exemplar in heaven.[97]

And there is even more evidence. The *Ibn Masud Codex* (from Kufa) is the version of the Qur'an used by Sunni Muslims, but is different from the standard text used by other Muslims. There are more than 150 variants in sura 2 alone! Because it is now too late to homogenize the text—because there is more than one version in use—Muslims simply ignore the problem. They claim that all Qur'ans are the same, as though that deals with the problem. L. Bevan Jones sums it up:

"... while it may be true that no other work has re-
mained for twelve centuries with so pure a text, it is
probably equally true that no other has suffered so
drastic a purging."[98]

In fact, no one possesses the original Qur'an, nor does
anyone even have a copy of the official Uthmanic text. The oldest copies of the Qur'an in existence are from a century and a
half after Muhammad. Considering one more piece of evidence,
the Arabic words on the outside of the Dome of the Rock do not
match any known version of the Qur'an! In short, there is no
single "pure" Qur'an. There are, rather, multiple versions, in
spite of the claim—which is really more like a conspiracy—that
the Qur'an has never been changed.

The Bible is *not* corrupt, despite Muslim allegations (see
5:13–15). It is the Qur'an that *has* been changed. Ironically,
its copyists, and Muslim leaders, have been guilty of doing the
very things of which they have accused the Christians! If you
want to study this further, spend some time in the excellent
work by Geisler and Saleeb, *Answering Islam.*[99]

10. Hadith (Tradition)

The Hadith are the traditions of Islam outside the Qur'an,
recorded in the collective experience, writing, and practice of
the Muslim community. Every religion tends to expand over
time. Judaism has the Mishnah and the Talmud. Islam has
the Hadith.

Judaism started with just the scriptures of the Old Testament, which they called the "Tanakh."[100] Over the course of
time, Jews began to collect writings of rabbis. These rabbinic
commentaries, records of differing interpretations on the application of Torah to everyday life, became known as the Mishnah.[101] The Mishnah was codified around 200 AD, and then
expanded with further commentary in the Talmud. The Palestinian and Babylonian Talmuds were probably completed

by 400 AD. Thus today the Jewish writings are significantly more extensive than just the original scriptures of the law, the prophets, and the writings.

Christianity started out with the Hebrew Bible, and soon added the apostolic accounts and letters. But over time, churches devised creeds, which became tests of fellowship. Historically, movements and organizations gravitate to defining themselves by documents. Creeds and councils, the decrees of synods, the declarations of the popes—all maintain uniformity and control. One thing is added to another, and eventually tradition rules.

This is exactly why Muslims pray *five* times a day. I often ask Muslims why they pray five times daily. They always answer, "The Qur'an tells me to." To which I respond, "I have read the whole Qur'an, and it's not in there. It must be in the Hadith." In fact, during a frank discussion with an imam, he told me that my understanding was on target. While five daily prayer times can be read into the Qur'an, the requirement is not explicit until the Hadith.

As mentioned earlier, when you ask a Muslim if he has read the Qur'an, you will typically get the same answer you get when you ask a Christian if he has read the Bible.

The typical Christian will say, "Well, I should read it more."

"So, have you read the whole thing once?"

"Well, um, portions of it..."

This means that people are trusting someone else to tell them what their Scriptures say and mean, rather than reading for themselves. Why is this important?

Every religion tends to go through expansions—and people seldom object, perhaps because they weren't reading their own Scriptures to begin with. Religions shift from the original doctrine—the teaching of the founder—to traditions, supplemented by the consensus and decrees of councils.

This is precisely what happened with Islam as it evolved from the Qur'an into the Hadith. Most Muslims follow the many Hadith, rather than the Qur'an.

In studying Islam, you learn of many practices and traditions. The practice of circumcision is one of these, five daily prayers another. Opening the Qur'an, you seek scriptural support for them in vain. *Hadith trumps Qur'an.*[102]

11. Is the Qur'an Really "Clear"?

While I would not go so far as Edward Gibbon, who complained about its "endless incoherent rhapsody of fable and precept," or Thomas Carlyle, who said that it was "as toilsome reading as I ever undertook; a wearisome, confused jumble, crude, incondite," I do agree that the Qur'an is not easy reading. And yet over and over the Qur'an insists that it is an *inspired* revelation from Allah, and that it is *clear.*

> Allah thus makes clear to you His messages that you may understand (2:242).

> We have made some of these messengers to excel others. Among them are they to whom Allah spoke, and some of them He exalted by degrees of rank. And We gave clear arguments to Jesus son of Mary, and strengthened him with the Holy Spirit... (2:253)

> And this Qur'an is not such as could be forged by those besides Allah, but it is a verification of that which is before it and a clear explanation of the Book, there is no doubt about it, from the Lord of the worlds (10:37).

We are tediously reminded of its "clarity" (22:16; 29:49; 57:9, 25). I suppose the Qur'an is quite "clear" about the sin of idolatry, the need to practice what you preach, and several other matters. And yet *the vast majority* of the Qur'an is difficult to read, and keeps even its own scholars guessing.

- Most passages lack a context.
- The arrangement is not chronological.

- The cultural separation between our time and Muhammad's is enormous.
- Later passages are often said to abrogate (update) earlier ones.[103]
- Allusions to biblical events are made with little or no explanation.

For example, the Qur'an mentions Abraham over one hundred times: 2:124–132, 133, 135, 140, 258; 3:64–67, 83; 4:125; 6:75–84; 9:114; 11:69–76; 12:6; 14:35–41; 15:51–60; 16:120–123; 19:41–49; 21:51–72; 22:26–29; 26:69–89; 29:16, 17, 24–27; 37:83–113; 38:45–46; 43:26–28; 51:24–34; 57:26; 60:4. Every passage *assumes* the reader already knows who this man is, and is familiar with all the key events in his life.

In contrast, the Old Testament account of Abraham spans Genesis 11–25. Nothing is assumed; we are introduced to the man and take in a stereoscopic view of this life. We get a feel for his strengths and weaknesses, his great faith and why he is such an important figure biblically. Abraham is a real person, with texture and depth. By comparison, the Qur'anic treatment is flat.

12. Jesus Christ

The first time I read the Qur'an, I was struck by how frequently Jesus Christ is mentioned. He appears far more often than Muhammad! Muslims have a high opinion of Jesus Christ. (Yet make no mistake, regardless of the word count, *Muhammad* is the central figure of the Qur'an, not Christ!) Muslims do not, however, agree with everything that Christians believe. What does the Qur'an teach about Jesus?

To begin with, he was a messenger, a prophet from God, who brought the gospel.

The Messiah, son of Mary, was only a messenger; messengers before him had indeed passed away... (5:75).

We made Our messengers to follow in their footsteps,
and We made Jesus son of Mary to follow, and We gave
him the Gospel... And We put compassion and mercy
in the hearts of those who followed him" (57:27).

Next, he was only a servant (43:59), not God in the flesh.
And yet, startling to most Christians, sura 19 teaches that he
was born of a virgin—that no man had touched Miriam, his
mother. She conceived the child by the power of God.

As we discussed earlier, the Qur'an also teaches that although Jesus was a prophet, he was not the son of God or God
in the flesh.

The Qur'an also refers to the miracles of Jesus. However,
his crucifixion and resurrection are denied. In the view of Islam, a shameful death like crucifixion would have been a sign
that Jesus was rejected by God. This view is similar to the Jewish perspective. The crucifixion is flatly denied: "That they said
(in boast), 'We killed Christ Jesus the son of Mary, the Messenger of Allah'; but they killed him not, nor crucified him, but
so it was made to appear to them, and those who differ therein
are full of doubts, with no (certain) knowledge, but only con-
jecture to follow, for of a surety they killed him not:—Nay, Allah raised him up unto Himself; and Allah is Exalted in Power,
Wise" (4:157-158).

In addition, Muslims unanimously reject the resurrection
of Christ. Instead, they affirm that he was taken up to heav-
en.[104] "And for their saying: We have killed the Messiah, Jesus,
son of Mary, the messenger of Allah, and they killed him not,
nor did they cause his death on the cross, but he was made to
appear to them as such" (4:157).

And yet Muslims acknowledge Jesus' second coming
(4:159; 43:61). They believe that Judgment Day will begin when
Jesus Christ returns and initiates the resurrection of the dead.
He will come back to the earth, to Jerusalem.[105] Now that is an
incredible conversation starter—"So what do you think about
Jesus' second coming?"—if you are reaching out to a Muslim!

So it is not true that Muslims fail to appreciate Jesus in every
respect. They do appreciate a number of biblical truths. But

when they deny Jesus' divinity, crucifixion and resurrection, they are rejecting the central teachings of Christianity (the incarnation and the atonement).

Since Muslims do not acknowledge the biblical plan of redemption, how do they deal with sin? In the Islamic faith, there is no atonement—no sense of God entering our world, becoming one with us and dying to save us. In these important areas, Christianity diverges sharply from Islam.

Processing This Chapter

How can you process all this material? Allow me to share a few perspectives here. First, if you are a Christian and you believe in the Bible, make sure you know what you believe. Make sure you finish reading the Bible several times through. I would encourage you to read the Scriptures daily, aiming to master them. (And no, you never fully master the Bible; you never "arrive.")

But it will also pay to make time to examine the scriptures of Islam. Remember, the Qur'an is only eighty percent the length of the New Testament; you can complete it in a couple of months, just by reading a few minutes a day. Take notes and underline. Strive for understanding. Or if you are not prepared to read the entire Qur'an, perhaps aim to peruse some of the key suras. Either way, we will understand Islam much better, and connect with Muslims much more, when we gain a basic familiarity with their scriptures. Do you agree?

As you read, realize that what we find in the Qur'an—and in the scriptures of any religion—is not all wrong. How could it be? Let's revisit the analogy of the moon's reflection of the sun's light.

Only as we contemplate the word of God, the Bible, and the son of God, Jesus Christ, do we see the sun and its full intensity.[106] When we look at the institutions, philosophies, religions, and movements of man, we still see light, but it is a *reflected* light. It is like the light of the moon. So it is not surprising that the truth would appear in many unlikely places. Yet there is a huge disparity between *some* truth and *all* truth. There is a difference between being impressed by the light of the moon and being blinded and dazzled by the light of the sun.

Although we can find truth and wisdom in the Qur'an, the differences between the Qur'an and the Bible, between Islam and Christianity, are major. In the first, Christ is only a prophet; in the second, the focal point of all history. Hardly a minor difference! The more you read and study, the more obvious—and polarizing—the differences appear. And while we can appreciate insights and shared values in both religions, we cannot straddle the fence.

We must choose what we believe and whom we follow. As Elijah put it in 1 Kings 18:21, "How long will you waver between two opinions? If the Lord is God, follow him..."

4

Violence:
The Exception or the Rule?

"We didn't do this for ourselves, but for our religion. Our religion is being destroyed. Let this be a lesson to enemies of our religion."

—Confession of one of the Muslims who tortured and murdered three Christians at a Protestant publishing house in eastern Turkey, 2007

As I edit this chapter, today is 9/11, the seventeenth anniversary of that dark day in American history. Like most of you reading this book, I remember precisely where I was and exactly what I was doing when the terrorist attacks took place. My plane had landed in Washington, D.C. I hurried from the airport to the Tuesday morning church staff meeting where we had intended to plan our calendar for 2002.

We watched in helpless horror as first the World Trade Center and then the Pentagon were attacked by Muslim hijacker-terrorists. We were separated from our children, who were in school, and reports were being broadcast of more hijacked planes heading to our area. The planning meeting became a prayer meeting!

Many died that day in Washington, D.C. and New York. Every family we knew was connected somehow with somebody who perished—a family member, a neighbor, the parent of one our children's schoolmates. The entire week was a heavy one emotionally.[107] As part of a small group Bible study, I visited the Pentagon five or six times soon after the attacks; the sense of sobriety and urgency was palpable.

My neighbor was in the World Trade Center at the time of the attacks. Soon after my plane landed, I phoned his wife to check whether her husband was safe, and she told me the most incredible story.

On the morning of 9/11, he had been lecturing in Tower 1. His topic: Emergency Preparedness for Terrorist Attacks! When the class felt the impact of the initial collision (on Tower 2), they relocated to another building in the complex, from which they spied the second plane crashing into Tower 1. The lecture was cut short, but my neighbor stayed on the site for four more days, coordinating the medical teams and helping in any way he could.

In time, the fact became clear that the perpetrators of this atrocity were Muslim extremists, one and all. The horrific events of 9/11 changed our world, ushering in an era of terror, and straining anew the relations between Christians and Muslims. For many Americans, 9/11 has become the defining representation of the Islamic faith. When they hear the words *Islam, Muslim* or *Arab*, they think "terrorist," "violence," and "bloodshed." Fear-mongers are enjoying their heyday.[108]

As Bruce Feiler puts it, "September 11, 2001, was the day the Middle East came to America."[109]

And as the outspoken atheist and anti-religionist Sam Harris warns: "We must come to terms with the possibility that men who are every bit as zealous to die as the nineteen hijackers may one day get their hands on long-range nuclear weaponry. The Muslim world in particular must anticipate this possibility and find some way to prevent it. Given the steady proliferation of technology, it is safe to say that time is not on our side."[110]

Typical or Atypical?

So what is true? Is the radical hostility we saw on 9/11 typical of Muslims? Are all followers of the Crescent nothing more than bloodthirsty monsters bent on acts of savagery against the "infidels"?

Clearly we cannot deny the violence that so many have witnessed. Neither is it right to project a vengeful stereotype onto all Muslims. An honest man does not desire to believe ill of others against the evidence. So what is the evidence?

To be sure, a violent strain resides within Islam. (Arguably, a violent strain exists somewhere within nearly all human religions.) This is true despite sura 2:256: "There is no compulsion in religion—the right way is indeed clearly distinct from error." To adequately cover the subject of violence and Islam, we must examine the characteristics of shari'a law, and then take an in-depth look at jihad and terrorism.

Shari'a Law

The media frequently—and sometimes unfairly—reminds us of the draconian violence of the Islamic legal system, based on shari'a law. Islamic law attempts to take the principles of the Qur'an and shari'a to formulate a civil and criminal code. Shari'a law used to dominate in Muslim lands, but in many countries it survives only in family law.

Under shari'a criminal law, a thief's hand is chopped off, an adulterer is stoned to death, and a homosexual is executed instantly.[111] The following report comes from Afghanistan:

> The Taliban militia's supreme leader, Mullah Muhammad Omar, warned that the death penalty will be enforced against any Muslim converting. *Shari'a* law is in effect.[112]

The Taliban also became famous with its unconscionable half-time entertainment on the soccer field: the execution of adulterers and other criminals.

Shari'a law is in force in many nations today, including one of the major allies of the United States in the Arabian Peninsula, Saudi Arabia.[113] Private worship in homes is even forbidden for the million migrant workers. Whereas the Saudis were allowed to build a mosque near the Vatican in 1995, so far they have not reciprocated. Conversion to any other religion typically carries a death penalty. In 2008, the Iranian parliament proposed the death penalty for all apostates from Islam. (This is based on sura 2:217 and 4:89.) And in many places, *you* may be executed if you convert another person to Islam. In Africa, shari'a law has inspired bombing campaigns against schools and hospitals.

Take, for example, the British schoolteacher in the Sudan who was accused in 2007 of dishonoring the Prophet. What was her sin? She had asked her class to help name her daughter's teddy bear. The name they selected was "Muhammad." This act was felt by many Muslims to be tantamount to blasphemy. She was detained while her sentence was decided. If convicted, she could have received forty lashes, a stiff fine, and up to a year in prison. Some Muslims demanded that she be stoned for the offense. Western media coverage of her case was prolific.[114] Eventually she received a presidential pardon and returned home to the United Kingdom.

Or consider a Saudi woman recently sentenced to six months in prison and two hundred lashes (would she even survive such a severe flogging?). Her crime: being gang-raped. (Apparently, the woman's appearing in public was all the justification the rapists required!)[115]

Or how about the following headline, "Saudi man kills daughter for converting to Christianity":

> According to an August 12 (2008) report from Gulf News, a young Saudi woman was recently killed by her father after he discovered that she had converted to Christianity. The father, who is a religious police member of the Commission for Promotion of Virtue and

Prevention of Vice,[116] cut out his daughter's tongue and burned her to death following a heated debate about religion.

In an online blog entry written a few days before her death, the woman mentioned how her family had begun to suspect her religious beliefs. Her father is reportedly being investigated for an honor-related crime, which carries a significantly lesser sentence than murder.[117] —*Voice of the Martyrs*, August 2008

These extreme examples are, unfortunately, more common than we might expect. They likely reflect a deeper issue and pattern with Islam: a violence that is not only tolerated but often actively encouraged. Two facts emerge when we monitor the media's coverage of Islam:

The media emphasizes the negative in Islam. This may be attributable to the media's characteristic alarmism, which fuels and sustains a culture of fear. Yet, even though reportage may be slanted, *acts of abuse and hostility are not at all uncommon in places influenced by Islam.*

Often Muslims defend the penchant for violence among their radical fringe, saying that there are justifications for terrorism, that these radicals are uneducated, oppressed, and poor. But many of those who organize and promote Islamic terrorism are highly educated! Moreover, how do members of other religions respond to hardship? For example, Tibetan Buddhists have suffered severely, for fifty years, at the hands of the occupying Chinese forces, but have you ever heard of Tibetan Buddhist suicide bombers?

We must hold these two truths in tension if we genuinely seek to study the Muslim religion with an objective mindset. Yes, the media distorts and exaggerates, to the detriment of Muslims, but all the same, the religion, and especially its code of law, both contain a serious propensity toward hostility.

Jihad

Perhaps the most famous example of violence within Islam, in our world, is *jihad*. But most of us have a limited understanding of the concept. Jihad is the Arabic word for "struggle." The word does not necessarily entail warfare, though that is one of its definitions. A well-known citation proclaims, "We are now returning from the lesser jihad to the great jihad."[118] What did the writer mean? He was calling Muslims to return from the lesser jihad of battle, to the greater jihad of establishing justice. Both entail struggle. Even in peacetime, great effort must be exerted to establish righteousness.

The concept of jihad is much broader than holy war—expanding the Muslim faith through military means. Jihad is the struggle that all followers of Islam are called to endure as they try to do what is right, to obey Allah and to resist evil in the world. Yet sadly, terrorism has become the ugly face of Islam to many people. The suicide bombers[119] that you read about in the newspapers are *jihadis*. Many airplanes have been destroyed, schools burned down, churches torn down. The media has made us all too aware that large numbers of would-be bombers stand ready to take life in order to make a point—and many others are lining up to take the places of the suicide bombers who blow themselves up.

The media shows us these horrific scenes, and of course, it is tempting to think that this behavior and mindset represent all Muslims. Yet most Muslims I've met have been nothing like these extremists. For every combative or belligerent Muslim I have encountered, I have met a hundred who are as reasonable and peace-loving as anyone else. We must resist the stereotyping that comes so easily.

Nevertheless, acting as though there were no significant hostile streak in Islam, both in the past and in the present, would be dishonest. From the beginning, this religion has spread through bloodshed. The Muslim faith began to spread in earnest only when the sword was taken up, especially in Arabia, North Africa, and Western Europe (and centuries later in Central Asia, India, and Central Europe).[120]

Unfortunately, the pattern of violence did not stop there. Even in our own time, we read about many horrors perpetrated through Islam in Asia, Africa, and the Middle East. The example that follows is but one of many similar stories:

> On a Sunday morning in 1987, 13-year-old Kur Mach Kur sat in church in Makol Cuai, a small village in southern Sudan, when armed Muslim raiders burst in during the pastor's sermon. The raiders demanded that the pastor renounce his faith in Jesus Christ. The pastor refused and as Kur watched, the raider shot and then dismembered the man who moments before had been teaching from the Bible.[121]

We might like to believe this is a rare event, but we cannot if we follow the news. I subscribe to *Christianity Today*, a reliable source for world developments that affect Christians, and I visit Web sites that report persecution and martyrdom. I can confidently report that every month, in multiple places around the world, men and women die for their faith in Christ.[122] Who are they killed by? Almost always by Muslims, though also by Hindus, Buddhists, and atheist governments.[123]

When we objectively consider the extent of Islamic militarism and terrorism, it is difficult not to have a dark impression of Islam. The 9/11 hijackers don't represent what most Muslims desire; however, the hijackers do represent what *some* Muslims desire and are willing to die for.

Many Muslim or Muslim-majority nations are notorious for persecuting Christians.[124] These include but are not limited to: Afghanistan, Algeria, Azerbaijan, Bangladesh, Brunei, Cyprus (North), Egypt, Eritrea, Ethiopia, India, Indonesia, Iran, Iraq, Jordan, Kazakhstan, Kosovo, Kuwait, Libya, Malaysia, Mauritania, Nigeria, Pakistan, Saudi Arabia, Somalia, Sudan, Syria, Tajikistan, Tunisia, Turkey, Turkmenistan, and Uzbekistan.

In many Muslim lands, if you speak against Muhammad or the Qur'an, you will be jailed. In some places, you may even be executed. We have mentioned the *fatwa*—call for his death—issued in 1989 against Salman Rushdie: He was marked because in his book, *The Satanic Verses*, he pointed out that the original Qur'an had a short passage reflecting the pagan background of its time. For that, he was to be assassinated.

A more famous fatwa was issued by Osama bin Laden in February 1998. He declared,

> "For over seven years the United States has been occupying the lands of Islam and in the holiest of places, the Arabian Peninsula, plundering its riches, dictating to its rulers, humiliating its people, terrorizing its neighbors, and turning its bases in the peninsula into a spearhead through which to fight the neighboring Muslim peoples. We—with God's help—call on every Muslim who believes in God and wishes to be rewarded to comply with God's order to kill the Americans and plunder their money wherever and whenever they find it. We call on [you] to launch the raid on Satan's U.S. troops and the devil supporters allying with them... The ruling to kill the Americans and their allies—civilian and military—is an individual duty for every Muslim who can do it in any country in which it is possible to do it."

Here again we find a decree from a respected leader to go and kill the unbeliever, to kill the infidel. Radical Muslims are people who fervently believe in their cause. They are not about to back down. Not all Muslims are radicals, but those who are, are passionate enough to die, even to kill, for their cause.

Extremism

How can such extremism exist in the modern world? Only where one's worldview supports it. There is often severely simplistic either/or thinking in the minds of the Islamists.

Radical Islamists divide the planet into *Dar al-Islam* (the House of Islam) and *Dar al-Harb* (the House of War). Dar al-Islam is territory where Muslim governments are in control, ruling by Islamic law. Non-Muslims, called dhimmis, are permitted to live there by the gracious permission of their Muslim rulers. *Dar al-Harb* (the rest of the planet) is yet to be dominated, and is accordingly "the House of War." This is because a de facto (and perpetual) state of *jihad* exists. This holy war may be interrupted by truces (when appropriate). As a matter of practical necessity, Islamic regimes cannot afford to sustain continuous warfare against their non-Muslim neighbors. Yet the ultimate goal is clear: global domination. One day all the world will be in the House of Islam. Of course not all Muslims share this vision, but the minority who do wield considerable influence.

> Jim Jones, David Koresh and Meir Kahane do not typify Christianity and Judaism in the eyes of the civilized West, but those same eyes are prone to see Osama bin Laden and Mullah Muhammad Omar as typifying Islam.
> —Richard Bulliet, Columbia University

Many nations around the world are troubled by Islamic extremists. I have already mentioned Afghanistan, and Pakistan also comes to mind. Then there is Russia, with the problems in Chechnya. Many of the former Russian republics are heavily Muslim, and places like Kyrgyzstan and Uzbekistan have suffered because of extremists. For years India has faced difficulties with its Muslim population, as well as violence from some Hindus. When independence came in 1947 and the country was partitioned into India and Pakistan, millions lost their lives because of violence—Hindus killing Muslims, Muslims killing Hindus.

Certainly—and I think this bears repeating—we should not judge all Muslims by their worst representatives. As Columbia professor Richard Bulliet puts it, "Jim Jones, David Koresh and Meir Kahane do not typify Christianity and Judaism in the eyes of the civilized West, but those same eyes are prone to see Osama bin Laden and Mullah Muhammad Omar as typifying Islam."[125]

However, the strong violent tendency within Islam emerged even in the faith's nascence and continues to this day. If we care about the future, we will not ignore this truth.

Some Nations Troubled by Islamic Extremism

Afghanistan	Algeria	Australia	Bangladesh
Bosnia	Chechnya	Egypt	Ethiopia
France	India	Indonesia	Iran
Iraq	Israel	Jordan	Kyrgyzstan
Lebanon	Libya	Nigeria	Pakistan
Philippines	Russia	Saudi Arabia	Spain
Sudan	Syria	Tajikistan	Turkey
Turkmenistan	United Kingdom	United States	Uzbekistan

Some Westerners are guilty of thinking that all Muslims are terrorists. That stereotype, as we have seen, is blatantly false. However, I do give credence to the statement, "Almost all terrorists are Muslims." This claim may sound extreme, especially coming from a non-Muslim like me, but I am actually quoting the sincere admission of a peaceful, educated, and moderate Muslim.

The following words were penned by Saudi journalist Abdel Rahman al-Rashed. Notice his tone—the heavy heart, the pathos, the care, and the concern with which he writes:

"It is a certain fact that not all Muslims are terrorists, but it is equally certain, and exceptionally painful, that almost all terrorists are Muslims."

Powerful words. Yes, there are thousands of non-Muslim terrorists out there[126]—but we are not addressing those people in this book. We are tracing the salient patterns in Islam, and the Saudi journalist Abd al-Rahman al-Rashid has put his finger on the truth.

Western Culture

Many persons (both Muslims and "prophets" within Western culture) saw the events of 9/11 as God's judgment on the decadent West. I do not believe that God *directly* sent those airplanes into the Pentagon or the World Trade Center. And yet I have no doubt that God *allowed* the events of 9/11, because he either causes or allows everything that happens.

What made the perpetrators feel so justified in their actions? If you are part of Western culture, then you may not understand the mindset of the terrorists or those who approve of their actions. If you are not even *aware* of Western culture and its reputation, then you are definitely part of it.

Objectively understanding our own culture from within its narrow confines is nearly impossible.[127] Only when you begin to travel and live in other countries can you begin to see the way that the rest of the world views the West. Western culture is a mixture of good and bad, an amalgam of beauty and ugliness. We experience a freedom that is both wonderful and terrible. Western culture is decadent, and increasingly so. We who are parents have an obligation to educate our children and, especially in their early years, to protect them from this culture, with its destructive temptations and attitudes.[128]

The Islamic fundamentalists are reacting, in part, to this dissipation and worldliness. Their aim is not just power. They have a legitimate point when they talk about the corruption of the West. During the cold war, the Communists—and I am no Communist—would critique capitalism: People worship money and morals decline; morale slips; promiscuity, violence, and many other evils proliferate. And do you know what? They were right! Does this argument mean that their system is right? Certainly not, but they were right about the corrupting influence of money. (Jesus said the same thing, did he not?)[129]

We must listen to our critics, even our enemies, and acknowledge truth where it resides.

Palestine

No discussion of conflict within Islam can neglect the Palestinian controversy. Many Muslims are infuriated by what is going on in Israel. They see a very small state, created by Britain and the United States in 1948—six million Israelis, surrounded by a quarter of a billion Arabs. Even today, Israel is sustained as a viable nation by Britain and the U.S.

Can you guess which nation is the number-one recipient of U.S. foreign aid? One would think it might be a poverty-stricken nation full of starving refugees, like the Sudan or other parts of equatorial Africa. But no; for many years, the top recipient of U.S. foreign aid has been Israel.

I am not offering political advice about what the U.S. should do. I do not have the wisdom to counsel leaders on either side of what appears an intractable situation. I am simply pointing out that the Israeli-U.S. connection galls most Arabs. This alliance has undoubtedly led to hardship for the Arab peoples. (It is important to remember that Arabs are not all Muslim. Many Arabs are Christian, and some are Jewish, or follow other religions—though most are Muslim.)

Israel has been the thorn in the side of U.S.-Muslim relations for many years. Why do I mention this fact? Because to truly have the "big picture," we must try to look at the picture from the Palestinian angle, and with a degree of empathy.

First, the culture of the West—incarnate in the United States—is seen as corrupt, destroying families, eroding faith, and leading to its own idolatries (money, power, and more).

Then, understand that the Palestinians had lived in their homeland for a thousand years, and all of a sudden their homes were bulldozed or they were told to move, making them refugees in their own land. They have been surrounded by an unscalable wall, cut off from the rest of the Holy Land. And why?

As they see it, they were displaced because of a dubious claim based on the Bible, and because of the West's collective guilty conscience for allowing the Holocaust. Further, Arabs in the region continue to be afflicted because of the insatiable Western demand for oil—including *Arab* oil.[130]

I know I am treading on sensitive ground here, but it is much easier to demonize one side or the other rather than to actually look at the big picture. I urge us to have compassion on the Arabs and Muslims and to try to understand some elements of their viewpoint. Israel is a hot-button issue for most Arabs and Israelis alike. While I do not take sides, I appreciate the plight of persons on both sides. On a happier note, I have been deeply encouraged by my visits to Christian churches in Israel, where I have seen former Muslims and former Jews—former enemies—sitting together, laughing together, worshipping together, hugging each other. What a powerful testimony to the healing power of Christ, in a land that has seen so much division and so much violence.

Violence in the Qur'an

I am not backpedaling and defending the Muslims. I only share my observations about the motives of those who use Islam as a reason for violence. However, the Muslim religion itself was steeped in violence long before the Palestinian conflict served as a modern-day rallying point. Consider these passages from the Qur'an:

> But when the forbidden months are past, then fight and slay the idolaters wherever you find them, and take them, and prepare to ambush them. But if they repent and establish worship and they pay the poor due [the poor tax], then leave their way free (9:5).[131]

Or to paraphrase another passage, "Wage war on them until

the infidels are no more..." (9:29). Taking these and other passages at face value, we could even say that Muslims who deny the violence of the Qur'an, even those who reject violence, are in a way being disloyal to their own religion. At the very least, they are ignorant of their own religion.

All the way back in 622 AD, Muhammad fled Mecca for Medina. He declared jihad against all who would not follow him—not just against the idolaters, but against anyone who would not support him. What does the Qur'an say about martyrdom?

> So let those who fight in the way of Allah who sell this world's life for the Hereafter. And whoever fights in the way of Allah, be he slain or be he victorious, We shall grant him a mighty reward (4:74).

> Surely Allah has bought from the believers their persons and their property—theirs (in return) is the Garden. They fight in Allah's way, so they slay and are slain. It is a promise which is binding on Him in the Torah and the Gospel and the Qur'an (9:111).

Nor is there to be any turning back in battle:

> O you who believe, when you meet those who disbelieve marching for war, turn not your backs to them. And whoso turns his back to them on that day—unless maneuvering for battle or turning to join a company—he, indeed, incurs Allah's wrath and his refuge is hell. And an evil destination it is (8:15–16).

Jihad is often interpreted militarily:

> And fight with them until there is no more persecution, and all religions are for Allah... (8:39)

So when you meet in battle those who disbelieve, smite the necks [strike off their heads]; then, when you have overcome them, make (them) prisoners, and afterwards (set them free) as a favor or for ransom till the way lay down its burdens. That (shall be so). And if Allah please, He would certainly exact retribution from them, but that He may try some of you by means of others (47:4–6).

And those who are slain in the way of Allah, He will never allow their deeds to perish. He will guide them and improve their condition. And make them enter the Garden, which He has made known to them. (See also 22:58.)

Truly Allah loves those who fight in His Cause in battle array, as if they were a solid wall (61:4).

I will cast terror into the hearts of those who disbelieve. Therefore strike off their heads and strike off every fingertip (8:12ff).

If you are slain in Allah's way or die, then pardon from Allah and mercy are better than what they amass. For if you die or you are slain, truly to Allah you are gathered (3:157–158).

They who have fled their country and quit their homes and suffered in my cause, and have fought and fallen, I will blot out their sins from them, and I will bring them into gardens beneath which the streams do flow (3:194).

All these passages glorify martyrdom. If one dies in the service of Allah, he finds mercy, a "great reward." It is important to note that suicide bombers are acting in direct violation of the principles of Islam. Suicide, by most Muslims, is considered to be a serious sin. Others, however, justify violence, pointing to Samson as an example of legitimate suicide terrorism in the Bible. (In Judges 16:30, Samson, blinded and shackled, caused the Philistine temple to collapse, bringing about the death of three thousand.)

The Qur'an orders the punishment of enemies:

> The only punishment of those who wage war against Allah and his Apostle, and strive hard for mischief for the land is: execution, or crucifixion, or cutting off of hands and feet from opposite sides of the body, or exile from the land. This shall be a disgrace for them in this world, and in the Hereafter they shall have a grievous chastisement—except those who repent before you overpower them; so know that Allah is Forgiving, Merciful (5:33–34).

Summing up, the Qur'an declares that enemies are to be dealt with severely, by:

- Exile
- Amputation of limbs
- Execution, even crucifixion[132]

Violence in the Hadith

The traditions concerning Muhammad, concerning both his words and his deeds, are prolific. Quite a few of them commend violence:

> Allah's Apostle was asked, "What is the best deed?" He replied, "To believe in Allah and His Apostle." The questioner then asked, "What is the next? He replied, "To participate in Jihad in Allah's Cause."

> Jihad is your duty under any ruler, be he godly or wicked. A man came to Allah's Apostle and said, "Instruct me

as to such a deed as equals Jihad (in reward)." He replied, "I do not find such a deed."

A day and night fighting on the frontier is better than a month of fasting and prayer.

He who dies without having taken part in a campaign dies in a kind of unbelief.

Nobody who dies and finds good from Allah would wish to come back to this world even if he were given the whole world and whatever is in it, except the martyr who, on seeing the superiority of martyrdom, would like to come back to the world and get killed again.

Surely, the gates of paradise are under the shadows of swords.[133]

Thus it is fair to affirm that, consistent with the Qur'an itself, many of the Hadith encourage violence.

Retaliation

Retaliation is a natural human response to aggression or injustice, and is found in the Bible as early as Genesis 4:23 (the first Lamech's honor killing). It appears on the lips of Samson (Judges 15:11), in his unspiritual and immature exclamation, "I merely did to them what they did to me." The urge to vengeance also appears in many of the Psalms (3:7; 18:37, etc). And yet it is never justified in the Old or New Testament, merely held up to the light, thus exposing its violence and ugliness. In fact, there are a number of Old Testament texts that teach against retaliation (Exodus 23:4–5; Leviticus 19:18; Proverbs 25:21–22, etc).

But the Qur'an, in contradistinction to Jesus' teaching in Matthew 5, permits, and even justifies, retaliation (42:41):

Allah loves not the public utterance of hurtful speech, except by one who has been wronged. And Allah is ever Hearing, Knowing (4:148).

And kill not the soul which Allah has forbidden except for a just cause.... But let him not exceed the limit in slaying. (17:33).

That (is so). And whoever retaliates with the like of that with which he if afflicted and he is oppressed, Allah will certainly help him. Surely Allah is Pardoning, Forgiving (22:60).

A Call to Arms?

When we compare the teachings of Jesus Christ and those of Muhammad, we must now ask: Is violence *consistent* or *inconsistent* with the teaching of each religion's founder?

Muhammad authorized execution, maiming, exile, and many other acts of force and violence. The Islamic faith spread through bloodshed, and—unlike Christianity—this way of winning converts was not a perversion or corruption of true Islam that occurred centuries later; this violence took place from the outset. Is violence consistent or inconsistent with the teaching of Muhammad? It is *consistent.*

On the other hand, violence is absolutely inconsistent with the teaching of Jesus. The violent attitudes in the Qur'an stand in stark contrast to the commands of Christ. That may be an unpopular position to take, particularly in our fear-saturated society, when many want to manipulate the Bible in order to justify warfare—but it is the truth. The early Christians were actually forbidden to take up the sword. They were forbidden to kill their enemy. What does Jesus say in Matthew 5, in the Sermon on the Mount? He does not call his followers just to tolerate their enemies. He does not say to ignore them. He certainly does not say we can kill them. He commands us to pray for them and to bless them. The entire next chapter is devoted to an examination of Jesus' pacifist teachings.

Is violence consistent with the teachings of the founder?

ISLAM   CHRISTIANITY

Muhammad: Jesus:

YES   NO

You may be thinking, "Wait a minute! What about the Crusades? Didn't Christianity spread by warfare, too?"

The response that most thinking Christians would give is that the Crusades did not represent genuine Christianity. Not that it is right for us Christians to distance ourselves from the atrocities of the Crusades—because we all have enough prejudice, injustice, and sin in our own lives to keep us humble—but clearly the Crusades were carried out in direct conflict with the spirit of Christ. The Crusades were based on misguided, hateful thinking, and they were wrong—very wrong!

The Crusades occurred *a thousand years* after Christ, and represented a distortion of his teachings, promulgated by a corrupt church system.

"But,"—you might further object—"the Crusades are just the tip of the iceberg. Weren't Christians using violence in the seventh century, when Muhammad got Islam started? So Christian violence is old as the sun!"

Indeed, those who claimed to follow Jesus Christ had been resorting to violent tactics since the fourth century. But *Christian violence*, as we shall see in the next chapter, is a grievous oxymoron.

The Bottom Line

When we ask whether violence is consistent or inconsistent with true Christianity, the truth becomes plain. Violence was unacceptable to Jesus—but promoted by Muhammad. The violent reputation of Islam is in accordance with Muhammad's teachings, but wholly inconsistent with Jesus' commands.

The Muslim world is founded upon the teachings of a man whose own lifestyle was tainted by violence. Moreover, some of his teachings condone retaliation, vengeance and bloodshed. Of course, not all Muslim individuals are extreme in their passions or bent toward violence. However, Islam undeniably justifies and even encourages such attitudes and behavior. And while Muslim extremists are just that—*extreme* in their fervor and in the profanity of their acts—their terrorism speaks more loudly than the quiet lives of peaceful Muslims.

We must be careful not to generalize or to associate all Muslims with the outrages committed by a minority; but we must also be honest about the facts about Muhammad and his religion. Only through truthful evaluation and thoughtful consideration can we deal with one another respectfully and with understanding.

Response:
Turn the Other Cheek?

You have heard that it was said, "You shall love your neighbor and hate your enemy." But I say to you, Love your enemies and pray for those who persecute you.

—Matthew 5:43–44, RSV

Lest Christians begin to feel superior to Muslims, let me ask, How much do we—I am speaking to biblical Christians here—actually obey Jesus' difficult teachings about forgiveness and love of our enemies?

One thing I found shameful after 9/11 was the attitude Christians displayed toward their newly identified foes. After this day of shock and mourning, everyone in my community and around the nation seemed to become intensely patriotic. Outside house after house, flags were unfurled. But with the patriotism came resentment and animus towards anyone who even appeared to be Muslim. One of my Hispanic friends—mistaken for a "terrorist"—was showered with obscenities as he walked down the street near his home in Southern California.

Instead of prayer, I heard angry outbursts that bordered on bitterness and hatred. I visited various Christian churches and heard all the prayers, but no prayers were offered on the enemy's behalf. Petition was made for "our troops" and their victory, but not for the enemy troops. The deaths of *our* men and women in uniform were tragedies; their dead were just statistics. Is this really how God in heaven looks at the dead and (far more numerous) wounded on both sides?

With that in mind, we must not become self-righteous. Yes, the Qur'an is riddled with strong calls for violence, but when Christians do not obey Jesus Christ, are we any different?

A Vital Distinction

Before we go any further, I feel it necessary to make a vital distinction. From time to time we have all been inspired by accounts of bravery in battle. Every culture, after all, tells stories about its heroes. I too appreciate the virtues of those serving in the Army, Navy, Marines, Air Force, and Coast Guard. Courage, discipline, obedience, loyalty, and camaraderie are qualities that all followers of Christ admire and strive for.

Moreover, I appreciate the freedoms we enjoy in our country, and as a student of history am quite familiar with how they have been secured. My father served in the navy in World War II, just as his father served in the army in World War I. Though I was never in the armed forces, I did spend five years in an organization directly inspired by the military: the Boy Scouts. I found the requirements for advancement personally motivating—projects, merit badges, ranks, award—and went all the way to become an Eagle Scout (with palms).

Even today I know and respect many in the armed forces. I have been on numerous military bases, visited war memorials and cemeteries the world over, been inside the Pentagon and the White House multiple times, and spoken face-to-face with those actively serving, as well as with many retired from duty. I consider myself a good citizen: one who prays for his government, obeys its laws, pays his taxes and takes special care not to slander its leaders.

However, the subject of what the New Testament teaches about enemies is a *separate* issue. Questioning the use of violence is not a rejection of character, bravery, or the willingness to lay down one's life for one's friends (John 15:13; 1 John 3:16). This issue must be approached dispassionately if we are to hear what the Lord has said in this area. Once again, the rest of this chapter is not meant to be taken as a renunciation of courage, discipline, obedience, loyalty or camaraderie, or as a denunciation of all who in good conscience strive to do their part to promote freedom in the world. Rather, we are focusing now on one biblical matter: the use of violence in response to one's enemies. What Christ says about how we should view our enemies is not the same as what our government says on the matter.

Onward, Christian Soldiers?

Few Christian ministers or writers dare take a stand against *all* violence. But Jesus himself did just that. Listen to his words, taken from the end of Matthew 5, in a stretch of scripture commonly known as the Sermon on the Mount:

> You have heard that it was said, "An eye for an eye and a tooth for a tooth." But I say to you, Do not resist one who is evil. But if anyone strikes you on the right cheek, turn to him the other also; and if anyone would sue you and take your coat, let him have your cloak as well; and if any one forces you to go one mile, go with him two miles. Give to him who begs from you, and do not refuse him who would borrow from you.
>
> You have heard that it was said, "You shall love your neighbor and hate your enemy." But I say to you, Love your enemies and pray for those who persecute you, so that you may be sons of your Father who is in heaven; for he makes his sun rise on the evil and on the good, and sends rain on the just and on the unjust. For if you love those who love you, what reward have you? Do not even the tax collectors do the same? And if

you salute only your brethren, what more are you doing than others? Do not even the Gentiles do the same?
You, therefore, must be perfect, as your heavenly Father is perfect (Matthew 5:38–48, RSV).

What are Christians to do, according to Jesus, in respect
to our enemies?
- We are not to resist them. The Lord will judge them;
  this is not our duty.
- Like our Lord, we are to "turn the other cheek."
- We are not to hate them.
- We are to pray for them.

In these respects, we are to rise above the level of morality of
those who do not know God. We are to strive for perfection
(complete maturity), even as God is perfect. If Jesus spoke the
truth from God, is there room to hate our fellow man? *None at
all.*

During one of my debates with an eminent rabbi, my opponent searched for a weakness in my position. He affirmed
confidently, "Of course there's justifiable killing—not murder,
and the Bible makes a distinction here... [But] to be a pacifist
in the face of evil is to be complicit with evil..."

The rabbi then made an interesting distinction: "We're told
to love *our* enemy, but not to love *God's* enemy. Do you really
believe for a moment that Jesus wants you to *love* Hitler, or
love Osama bin Laden?... When [my evangelical friends] tell
me that Jesus wants them to love Osama bin Laden, I am just
in shock. Let me say it on the record: I *hate* Osama bin Laden.
I think he's a monster, a cruel monster who has desecrated
Islam, killed innocent people—and I *hate* him! Hatred has its
place—the Bible says clearly that hatred has its place. Hatred
is the appropriate godly response when confronted with true
irreversible wickedness..."

I suppose once we start distinguishing *our* enemies and
God's enemies (and what are the criteria for telling them
apart?), we are well on the way to rationalizing all kinds of hatred and violence.

The rabbi then asked me, "Douglas, do you love Osama bin Laden?"

I responded, "If you mean, do I have any amorous or affectionate feelings towards him, then no, of course not. But if you mean love in the *true* sense of the word—wanting the best for him, which in his case would be for him to repent—then yes, I would say I do."

Needless to say, my response did not satisfy the rabbi. The truth is, pacifism does not condone evil—far from it. Yet the Scriptures tell us, "Do not be overcome by evil, but overcome evil with good" (Romans 12:21). When bin Laden was killed, I did not rejoice in the streets. In fact, I recorded a podcast titled "Rejoicing in the Death of Osama bin Laden (?)" to provoke my listeners to think how Jesus would respond to the death of this terrorist.

Failure to Pray

To bring it home, during the war between the Allies and Iraq (beginning in 1991), as well as during the "War on Terror" of the George W. Bush presidency, I only once heard prayers for the enemy. (And that was because I spoke to the man concluding the service and asked him to remember the enemy.) If you attend church regularly, how often have you heard those leading the prayers mention "the enemy"?

The sad fact is that virtually *no* Christian congregations pray for the enemy. Why not? Because to do so would be deemed unpatriotic. But what about Jesus' words? What about his teaching on non-violence in the Sermon on the Mount? Was he unclear? Or have we so bought into the ideology of the state and the military machine that we no longer hear Jesus? How far we have drifted from the irenic and Christ-like spirit of our early brothers and sisters in the faith.

These may be challenging and painful words, and doubtless some of my readers will think me an ingrate and a coward. I will leave it to the Lord to judge the motives and attitudes of my heart.

Doublethink?

But we are called to a higher standard than just prayer for our enemies. You may ask: Are we even permitted to use force against our enemy? That appears to be out of the question for Christ's followers as well. When one of Jesus' disciples drew a sword to prevent his master's arrest, Jesus retorted, "Put your sword back into its place; for all who take the sword will perish by the sword" (Matthew 26:52).[134] In other words, Christians are not to take up arms.

Many Christians are of two minds about the use of violence. They instinctively know that it is wrong, and that the scriptures of the New Testament condemn it. And yet, bombarded continually by pseudo-religious justifications for warfare, they tend to succumb to the party line.

To illustrate, in an episode of the animated television series *South Park*, a character identified as Jesus makes an appearance. Using a bladed throwing star, he cuts one of the "bad guys" in half. Many conservative Christian leaders condemned *South Park* for blasphemy. Here is the irony: These are the same religious conservatives who view military service as an honorable calling for Christians. Does the Jesus-loving Navy Seal hesitate to cut the "bad guy" in half when he encounters him on some street in Baghdad?

As one Christian who viewed the episode put it, "The outlandish portrayal of Jesus as killing machine takes the pro-military Christians aback, even as they continue to insist that a good soldier can be a good disciple. It is a case of symbolism over substance in the extreme: Offended by a homicidal Jesus cartoon, but not by their own calls—in the name of Jesus—to commit homicide for God and country."[135]

The Record of Early Christianity

The truth is that active military service was forbidden in the early church, from its inception until the formation of the state-church in the 300s. Not until the fourth century, after the marriage between church and state, were Christians encouraged to fight in the army. Though a thorough exposition of this topic is beyond the scope of this book, anyone who wants to read the position held by the early church need only search the patristic writers. Following is a sampling of quotations from some of the best-known and most influential writers.[136]

- "We who formerly murdered one another now refrain from making war even upon our enemies." —Justin Martyr, c. 160 AD
- "We have learned not to return blow for blow, nor to go to law with those who plunder and rob us. Not only that, but to those who strike us on one side of the face, we have learned to offer the other side also." —Athenagoras, c. 175 AD
- "The Lord will save them in that day—even His people—like sheep... No one gives the name of 'sheep' to those who fall in battle with arms in hand, or those who are killed when repelling force with force. Rather, it is given only to those who are slain, yielding themselves up in their own place of duty and with patience—rather than fighting in self-defense." —Tertullian, c. 200 AD
- "Now inquiry is made about the point of whether a believer may enter into military service. The question is also asked whether those in the military may be admitted into the faith—even the rank and file (or any inferior grade), who are not required to take part in sacrifices or capital punishments... A man cannot give his allegiance to two masters—God and Caesar... How will a Christian man participate in war? In fact, how will he serve even in *peace* without a sword? For the Lord has taken the sword away. It is also true that soldiers came to John [the Baptist] and received the instructions for their conduct. It is also true that a centurion believed. Nevertheless, the Lord afterward, in disarming Peter, disarmed every soldier." —Tertullian, c. 200 AD
- "Wars are scattered all over the earth with the bloody horror of camps. The whole world is wet with mutual blood.

And murder—which is admitted to be a crime in the case of an individual—is called a virtue when it is committed wholesale. Impunity is claimed for the wicked deeds, not because they are guiltless—but because the cruelty is perpetrated on a grand scale!" —Cyprian, c. 250 AD

- "If, then, it is in no way permitted to commit homicide, it is not allowed for us to be present at all—lest any bloodshed should reach our conscience." —Lactantius, c. 304–313 AD

- "...When God forbids us to kill, he prohibits more than the open violence that is not even allowed by the public laws. He also warns us against doing those things that are considered lawful among men. For that reason, it will not be lawful for a just man to engage in warfare, since his warfare is justice itself. Nor is it lawful for him to accuse anyone of a capital charge. For it makes no difference whether you put a man to death by word, or by the sword instead. That is because it is the act of putting to death itself that is prohibited. Therefore, with regard to this commandment of God, there can be no exception at all. Rather, it is always unlawful to put a man to death, whom God has willed to be a sacred creature." —Lactantius, c. 304–313 AD.

No known Christian writing condoned military service until the fourth century. Rather, soldiers who converted to Christianity were required to refuse both oaths to the state and killing in all forms. Christians who joined the army were excommunicated. Some apparently were allowed to serve in peacetime in a "police" capacity.[137]

In time, of course, the church slowly evolved from pacifism to militarism:

- 170 AD—First record of Christians even being in the army, apparently converted after enlistment. Were not permitted to kill.

- 200s—Increased military service (frontiers of the empire).

- Late 200s—Christians were considered of more service to the realm through their prayers than if they fought in the legions. Still, Christians were (nearly) universally pacifist.

- 311—Attitudes changed once emperor and officials were on the side of the Christians.
- 300s—Christians in the army were forbidden to resign!
- 400—"Just War" theory formulated by Ambrose (340-397) and Augustine (354-430). This thinking argues that if one's cause is right, then violence is acceptable. It was an innovation in the fourth century; a commonplace idea today.[138]

The problem is not that Jesus' words were unclear, but that many Bible-centered churches have aligned themselves with the military. All too often, patriotism moves the hearts of church members even more than the evangelistic imperative of their Lord.

"Support the War"?

Evangelical Christians are often made to feel that, if they do not support the current war effort (whatever it may be at the time), they are being more than unpatriotic; they are disobeying the Scriptures. Every week I receive emails urging me to support the military, and directing me to websites that pressure believers to "support the war."

One pro-war website I recently visited offered only two scriptures in support of its position.[139] The first was Ecclesiastes 3:8, where Solomon's poem has the line, "a time for war." Yet Solomon is simply describing life as it is—and the life under the old covenant, at that. His poem was never meant to be a source for Christian doctrine. Moreover, Christians are not bound by the old covenant (see Ephesians 2:15, Colossians 2:14, and Hebrews 10:1, among others). The website went on to compare new covenant military service to the God-ordained wars against the Canaanites in the book of Joshua.

The second passage referenced by the site was Mark 13:7, where Jesus warns his followers, "When you hear of wars and rumors of war, do not be alarmed." But Jesus proceeds to tell his followers to "flee" (Mark 13:14), not to join in the fight, even though their homeland was being invaded by the Roman armies.[140] Thin support, indeed, for Christian military service.

Neither of these proof texts tells Christians to fight! Another website I visited made more of an effort to defend killing from the New Testament scriptures.[141] Luke 3 and Matthew 8 were cited in support of military service. In both examples, John the Baptist and Jesus interact with soldiers, but neither passage comments on whether killing is ethical. But then neither did he tell soldiers not to engage in idolatry, which was also usually entailed in military service. Besides, arguments from silence—"Jesus never told them not to kill"—are logically weak (if not fallacious).

Then the site presented Matthew 10:34: "...I did not come to bring peace, but a sword." But the sword Jesus refers to is not literal, but metaphorical, as a cursory glance at verse 35 makes clear. The sword to which Jesus refers is the division of relationships, as an inevitable consequence of the gospel—not the "division" of bodies by the weapons of war.

A reference to Luke 22:36-38 came next: "If you don't have a sword, sell your cloak and buy one." And yet when Peter took Jesus literally, Jesus corrected him; and when he drew his sword to defend his friend (in Matthew 26:52, the parallel passage to Luke 22:49–51), Jesus famously commented, "Put your sword back in its place, for all who draw the sword will die by the sword."

Last, this site referenced John 2:15, where Jesus made a whip out of cords, and challenged the money-changers in the Temple courts. "The Greek language implies that he used the whip on the money changers as well as on the sheep and oxen. Physical force can be applied with justice." But the Greek implies nothing of the kind. Nor does the context, as most commentators agree.

All evangelicals appeal to the Scriptures to support their position—whether pro—or anti-war—but both sides cannot be right. I encourage the thoughtful reader to carefully weigh the Scriptures.

Cowardice?

I am inspired by a brother in Christ, R. B. Scott, a man of conviction whom I met in the early 1980s while I was living in London. At that time he was already nearly ninety years of age. During one memorable conversation, we began talking about some of the hard times Europe has experienced. The subject came around to the war.

I asked, "Did you fight in the War? I mean World War I, of course." I was unsure how he would answer.

"No, I did not."

"Then what did you do during those years?"

"I was in prison. Wouldn't fight, so I got into trouble with the government."

"Where did they put you?"

"Wormwood Scrubs." (Wormwood Scrubs is a notorious prison in west London.)

"How long?"

"A couple of years. I couldn't kill. It wouldn't have been right."

I admire the *courage* of a man like that.

> "What difference does it make to the dead, the orphans, and the homeless, whether the mad destruction is wrought under the name of totalitarianism or the holy name of liberty and democracy?"   —Mahatma Gandhi

But Does Pacifism Work?

Some will doubtless object that pacifism is not practical. While we should not choose our Bible interpretations on pragmatic grounds, I would still strongly counter that argument. The entire Bible is full of warnings not to put our trust in military power, governments, treaties, or the "arm of flesh."[142] We ignore such warning signs at our own peril.

Besides, even if all followers of Christ decided to take their Lord at his word, and not kill their enemies, that would hardly pose a threat to global politics. Nations will continue to wage wars to impose their will, protect their assets, and gain access to resources. It is my conviction that one Christian on his knees far better serves his country than a thousand killing the enemy.

Many Bible believers have unthinkingly assumed that power politics and the war machine can be aligned with the will of God—that somehow this warmongering pleases him. But forcing our will on others is quite unlike the way of God, who in his "modesty" (as some theologians note) leaves us to make our own decisions.[143] There are significant and compelling arguments for this position, and many theologians and students of the Bible[144] share this viewpoint.

Perhaps more important, pacifism has been shown to work. Just consider the phenomenal success of such pacifist leaders as Mahatma Gandhi and Martin Luther King, Jr. Or the work of Greg Mortensen in building schools in Pakistan and Afghanistan, in the conviction that education is far more effective a strategy for combating militant Islam than warfare.[145] The track record of peace is considerably stronger than the record of warfare. Ron Sider persuasively argues that pacifism works—and yet our first instinct is to turn to arms:

"If top global Christian leaders (hopefully joined by Jews, Muslims, Buddhists, and others) led a thousand people into the West Bank, the eyes of the world would be on them. Hundreds of millions would be praying for peace and justice for both Israelis and Palestinians. Massive media coverage would pressure both sides to negotiate. The same would happen if Archbishop Tutu led a few thousand praying African Christians, joined by people from other continents, into Zimbabwe to demand that President Mugabe call fair elections... Nonviolence has worked. It's time to invest large amounts of money and time in serious training and deployment. We cannot know ahead of time what will happen. But we already know that unless we do this, our Christian rhetoric about war will be both hypocritical and dishonest."[146]

Pacifism is not quietism (saying nothing, doing nothing). Pacifism is overcoming evil by good. In short, pacifism does not undermine the cause of truth. It is even more effective than coercion and violence. It works![147]

Questions

As an international speaker and writer, I receive thousands of emails every year. A number of them center round the issue of whether it is permissible for Christians to resort to violence. Since relatively few Bible believers are pacifists, these interchanges may help others who are thinking through the issues. Following are five questions I received, along with my responses. The questions (edited for clarity) are in italics; the responses follow.

(1) Was Jesus' intention in Matthew 26:52 ("Put your sword back in its place... for all who draw the sword will die by the sword") that the sword be "taken" from all Christians, in regard to all military action, or just in the context of preventing the crucifixion? I joined the army after I became a Christian, just for the great college benefits and a little adventure. Since that time, I've moved up in the ranks and have become a sniper. It is a prestigious position, but naturally I've been conflicted over passages like Matthew 5 and 26. I am well aware of what I'm being trained to do, but is this really contrary to the teaching of Jesus? Isn't there "a time for war" (Ecclesiastes 3:8)?

Thanks for your question. It is a good one, and an important one. And maybe not one on which all thinking Christians will agree. My understanding of the texts, as well as of the quotes from early church history, is that all killing is forbidden. Ecclesiastes 3 of course refers to life under the old covenant. And yet even if there is "a time to kill," that would not mean that this is approved of, or that Christians are permitted to take part. Proverbs and Ecclesiastes often simply observe things the way they are. As you think through this issue, I would suggest you read Driver's helpful book *How Christians Made Peace with War*.

(2) In many of the Q&As at your website, you suggest that it is wrong to take up arms against your oppressors. What does that make of the Mandelas of Africa, and other liberation movements?

Mandela effected real change only after being imprisoned and renouncing violence, isn't that right? The real question is, What did Jesus say about how we are to treat our enemies? How do you read this?

I agree about how we are to treat our enemies as Christians. I suppose the whole concept of "freedom" from oppression or bondage means one experiences some violence of some sort. But how would Christian Europe protect or rid itself of Nazism if not by violence? Is it practical to "do a Gandhi" in all cases? What if the other cheek is "crushed"—do we turn the other to get "crushed" also? I do wrestle with this issue.

We cannot be certain a "Gandhi" would have worked against Hitler. However, what governments do is very different from what individual Christians do. (You and I are not states, are we?) The ancient church believed that their prayers were of far greater value against the enemy than killing. So even if all true Christians refused to kill Nazis, that doesn't mean Hitler would have won. Given how few churchgoers are true disciples of Christ, almost the same number of people would still have fought on the Allied side. But the war might have been shorter! (What a thought!)

(3) My husband is in the army. There have been periods when we've wondered what would be more pleasing to God, to reenlist or to get out. In the churches we've attended, people don't see any contradiction between being a disciple of Christ and a soldier. I get the sense when reading your various Q&A segments on this subject that you are against taking up arms. I agree with you, yet I must admit it's very challenging, since this is our livelihood. Did Jesus really forbid taking up arms?

Yes, this is a big decision. It affects your family and your income—but also your conscience and your relationship with God. Jesus forbade hating one's enemy (Matthew 5:43–44), and even resisting an evil person (Matthew 5:39). Serving in the army is one thing, but killing is another. Do you agree?

The historical record is clear that the early church was pacifist. They understood Jesus to be forbidding murder (private killing) as well as warfare (collective killing). I believe they were correctly interpreting their Lord's words. It is the modern church that has neglected Jesus' teaching regarding enemies.

(4) Serving in the army is one thing, but killing is another. Nevertheless, isn't putting oneself in the position to potentially kill also wrong, or at least unwise? Not all military personnel are in jobs requiring them to carry arms, or to shoot. But often they're still in dangerous situations where they have to carry a gun. My husband has been in Iraq and Afghanistan many times. I have often asked him if he has shot anyone, and he says he's "not sure." (He'd fired his gun, but wasn't sure he'd hit anyone.) In the church that we were a part of, the advice was always, "As long as you don't harbor hatred toward that person, you aren't sinning." But I don't know about that—is it really biblical?

This is all very perplexing and frightening. For this reason my husband recently chose a job that did not require him to carry a weapon. Last, how can we reach other military soldiers and family members for Christ? Most are very proud of their family members' service, and aren't pacifists. They believe the service rendered is helpful and proactive. I guess what concerns me the most is that I want my thinking to line up with the Bible, and I am afraid that maybe it doesn't. This issue seems to have so many different viewpoints, and everyone has an opinion. Please help.

Yes, everyone has an opinion. But what did Jesus teach? Most modern churches need to rethink their politics. We are not ancient Israel, with a commission to eradicate the godless Canaanites. Nor are we a nation, only very small minorities within our nations. It doesn't matter how inconvenient or unpopular the truth is. We need to obey regardless.

Many military families will respect your convictions. Others will call you cowardly, unpatriotic, or worse. Yet we can never win people to the truth by compromising the truth. It is they who must change their minds (and conduct); the gospel requires no adjustments.

As far as non-combatant service, I see no problem with this at all. As long as the government does not demand your unconditional allegiance, or require you to violate scripture, many forms of service are surely acceptable. I think your husband made a wise decision. Anytime we violate conscience, we are treading on dangerous ground (James 4:17; Romans 14:23). I commend your willingness not to "follow the crowd in doing wrong" (Exodus 23:2).

(5) I've thought a lot about this issue, it greatly stresses me all the time. I have an obligation to my soldiers, my country, and legally, my contract I've sworn to. It's solely because of this obligation that I feel I've been making excuses in regard to Jesus' teaching. I had thought that the context of Jesus' teaching (especially Matthew 5:21, 38, 43) was everyday civilian life. Unfortunately, the only military context is found under the old covenant, but the kingdom was a physical one then. So now, I have to admit there is just no kingdom (or country) to defend here on earth. How futile a life is that! It angers me that I've fought

*for promotions, recognition, and positions out of selfish ambi-
tion—only to realize that I have walked into a dead end, and
maybe worse than a dead end! If I fall under Stop/Loss for our
2009 deployment, I'll be serving in a Recon element, sniper position for sixteen months in Afghanistan. We will occupy southern
Afghanistan, conducting patrols in an area that has radically
turned militant in the last few months. I could face a court mar-
tial for refusing to go. Now what do I do? This is a very stressful
situation.*

You are in a tight spot. You put it well: "There is just no
kingdom (or country) to defend here on earth." Sometimes we
do need to make a choice. Trust in the Lord, and be sure to
follow your conscience and your understanding of the word of
God.

Conclusion

Too many of us have bought into violence as an acceptable
response to our enemy, despite the teachings of Jesus Christ.
Clearly not all Christians have gone down this path, and these
words are not aimed at those who have shown grace and mercy
towards their enemies; these Christ-like souls are an upward
call to the rest of us. Yet the Scriptures are clear. Our patent
lack of love for the enemy—may I say the Muslim enemy?[148]—
violates the entire spirit of the Sermon on the Mount. Yes, the
Muslims must contend with violence and extremism within
their own camp, but we Christians must also grapple with our
own resentments and tendency toward retaliation. Let us neither minimize the threat from militant Islam *nor* fail to love
every man, be he friend or foe—or terrorist.

Unless *Christians* change their own hateful and militaristic attitudes and are willing to walk more closely with our Lord,
we cannot hope to build a bridge to the Muslim world.

6

Connections:
Reaching Out to Muslims

Though I am free and belong to no one, I have made my-
self a slave to everyone, to win as many as possible...
I have become all things to all people so that by all pos-
sible means I might save some.

—1 Corinthians 9:19, 22b NIV

G iven all the conflict and challenges in Christian-
Muslim relationships, is there any hope for recon-
ciliation, or even peaceful coexistence? Is it real-
istic to think a Christian can help a Muslim come to faith
in Christ?

I believe it is possible—indeed, I *know* it is possible, because I have seen it happen. For example, in 2007 I addressed
a church in Freetown, Sierra Leone. The majority of the audience had been converted from Islam, just as the majority of
the visitors—who nearly outnumbered the church members—
were Muslim. Hundreds and thousands of Muslims are finding
Christ! I myself have shared my faith with many Muslims, have
led some of them to repentance and baptism, and will continue
to do so.

Christ urges us to build bridges of peace with all human-ity, with no disqualification on religious grounds—any more than on grounds of gender or ethnicity! The apostle Paul urged, "If it is possible, as far as it depends on you, live at peace with everyone" (Romans 12:18). He modeled how to accomplish this difficult command as he connected with people, including skeptical and even hostile crowds, in a variety of settings: from synagogues to the Acropolis, where the Greeks worshiped a plurality of gods; to jailhouses; and even to the inner sanctums of the rulers of his day. Many of us do not fully appreciate all that Paul did to spread the gospel. Looking at the examples of Paul, Jesus, and the early Christians helps us to conclude our study on a positive, proactive note—one of hope, rather than of fear or despair.

Moreover, remember that Jesus charges his followers to take the gospel to *all* nations[149] (Matthew 28:18–20). So how can we begin to share our faith with the Islamic peoples and with our own Islamic neighbors?

Before we begin building bridges, we must first of all un-derstand the many differences between our two faiths—the points that cannot be made to harmonize. Glossing over the differences as though they are not significant does not help. In fact, it is insulting to our faith and theirs. But our faiths do share some points of agreement, and it helps to know where our beliefs overlap. These understandings are but the begin-ning of preparation for an intellectual connection with a mem-ber of the Islamic faith.

Next, it is wise to prepare ourselves to address the lines of reasoning that a Muslim is likely to use—assuming, of course, that he or she is motivated to defend his or her faith in an effort to convince us.

Third, we will improve our competence if we consider how to communicate certain key Christian concepts to our Muslim friends.

1. *Know Your Stuff*

Let us review and summarize the differences between the two faiths, in the light of evangelism. Clearly understanding our points of diversion will enable us to enter into meaningful dialogue with our Muslim neighbors. You may be unable to remember all the things you have read in the book so far. Don't worry! But it would be good to review the following points and make sure you have a general grasp of them.

A. As we read in the last chapter, one of the major differences between Christianity and Islam is what their respective scriptures teach about *violence*. Violence in Islam is consistent with the teaching of its founder, Muhammad, while it is inconsistent in the case of Jesus and Christianity.

B. Another key point of difference is the *ultimate* goal of the two religions. In Christianity, fellowship with the Lord and with one another is the ultimate goal. In Islam, the reward for adherence to its precepts is paradise, a sensual place. This promise is what motivates the martyrs. Many are told that if they die for Allah, they will receive the reward of seventy-two virgins.[150] They will have all the sex they want to have in paradise. This reward for martyrdom extends a powerful motivation for suicide bombers—usually young men in their teens or early twenties whose adolescent hormones are hyperactive, and who have spent years stifling their sexual desire. Yet these martyrs are promised more than just reward for themselves. Some are taught that up to seventy members of their families will go to paradise instead of to hell, by virtue of their sacrifice. In many places, after their deaths, their families receive cash payments, in addition to tremendous honor, because their son (or, more rarely, their daughter) chose to be martyred for Allah.

C. Yet another difference between the faiths is cultural. Whereas Christianity "works" anywhere, in any culture on the planet, Islam is *culturally bound*. As one book put it, Islamism is a form of cultural imperialism.[151] That is, the culture of seventh-century Arabia has been raised to the status of divine law. But shari'a law is impractical in most parts of the world. Not all societies are patriarchal. Individualism is the norm in the West, not collectivism (where attitudes are formed and actions are taken more by groups than by individuals). Some Muslim morals and mores are antithetical to those of other faiths and cultures.

D. Islam also diverges from Christianity in its scriptural *accuracy.* In our examination of the Qur'an, we saw many errors in its biblical references. Not every Qur'anic reference to biblical events is wrong, but there are mistakes galore. Some of these errors may be deliberate adjustments, others the result of Muhammad's learning the Bible through sectarian representatives of Christianity.

E. Another point to emphasize in our discussions with Muslims is the *nature of God.* Allah is not the God of the Bible. In the Qur'an, Allah is aloof. Sura 51:56 has Allah proclaim, "And I have not created the jinn and the men except that they should serve me." The Muslim god is grand, exalted, lofty, and far above humans. He has no direct contact with man, as does the God of Christianity. Muslims see themselves as subject to the mercies of fate, or *kismet.*

This point deserves further exploration. In contrast to Allah, the God of the Bible is referred to as being *spirit* in both the Old Testament and the New Testament. God is spirit, and those who worship him have to worship him in spirit (John 4:24), yet the Qur'an denies this fact, since Allah is conceived in physical terms.

While the God of the Bible is personal, in sharp contrast the god of the Qur'an is impersonal. The God of the Bible is knowable, while the god of the Qur'an is unknowable. To be sure, God's ways are beyond tracing out and his mysteries unfathomable (Romans 11, Isaiah 55). God is unknowable if that means having an exhaustive and comprehensive knowledge of God. In that sense, he is unknowable. But the Bible emphasizes over and over again that God is knowable and that he delights in making himself known to us. While we do not know him comprehensively or exhaustively, we do know him adequately. We know him personally, as a father and friend.

Let me repeat these three differences: In the Bible, God is a *personal, knowable spirit,* but in the Qur'an, he is not a spirit at all. Allah has a body. He is impersonal and no one can know him. Whereas in Christianity God is love (1 John 4:7), orthodox Muslims do not make such a claim.[152]

These are enormous, polarizing differences. Do not tell a Christian he worships the same god as the Muslims, and do not tell a Muslim he worships the same God as Christians! The differences are irreconcilable.

God of Bible Versus Allah

God of Bible	God of Qur'an (Allah)
Spirit	Not Spirit
Personal	Impersonal
Knowable	Unknowable

F. One last distinction concerns the issue of salvation by *grace* versus effort. In suras 40:9, 39:61, 7:43, and in many other locations, the Qur'an says that we earn grace, merit, favor, and paradise. Christianity, however, is founded upon salvation by grace (Ephesians 2:5). Works are proof of one's right standing with God (Ephesians 2:8–10; Titus 2:11–14; 1 Corinthians 15:9–10), but they do not in and of themselves make us right with God.

To sum up the differences, there are a number of fundamental points of departure: grace, the nature of God, scriptural and historical accuracy, the Islamic concept of a sensual paradise, and violence. We must appreciate these differences in order to build bridges with Muslims. That is, we need to "know our stuff."

A bridge is of no use unless each end is firmly anchored. If it is not anchored, how can you cross to the other side, or how can the person on the other side cross to you? Two supports are required in order to have a beneficial discussion. We need to know what we believe, and we also need to know what *they* believe. Sooner or later, each point of divergence will have to be discussed.

One way to build bridges is to engage in public dialogue. In 2008 I participated in a three-way public debate with a rabbi and an imam. Though naturally there were many points on which we disagreed, the event was conducted with true respect. In 2011 I was invited to speak at two universities in Bangladesh. In dialogue (not necessarily agreement) with a number of eminent Muslim scholars, I had the opportunity to show a different face of Christianity—hopefully one that combined Christian conviction with genuine respect.

Making genuine connections requires us, in the words of James 1:19, to "be quick to listen, slow to speak."[153] We desperately need more of that spirit in Christian-Muslim relations.

2. Emphasize What We Have in Common

Christians and Muslims share many common beliefs, and these points of agreement can serve as springboards to profitable discussion.

A. Revelation in a Book

Both Muslims and Christians believe that God has revealed his will to mankind in a book. In sura 2:136–7, we read,

> Say: "We believe in Allah, and the revelation given to us and to Abraham, Ishmael, Isaac, Jacob, and the tribes, and that given to Moses and Jesus and to (all) prophets and their Lord: We make no difference between one and another of them: And we bow to Allah (in Islam)." So if they believe as ye believe, they are indeed on the right path.

The Muslims embrace the idea that God revealed himself not just to the great men and women of faith of the Old Testament, but also to Jesus. They believe in one god. They acknowledge that the biblical God gave a written word to Moses, and that it served as a guide for the children of Israel. The Qur'an promotes a high view of the Old and New Testament.

B. *Submission*

Another point of commonality is the emphasis on submission. Throughout the Bible, Christians are told to submit to God (for example, see Hebrew 12:7–11 and also James 4:7). Remember that "Islam" means submission. Consider this passage:

> When Jesus found unbelief on their part He said: "Who will be my helpers to (the work of) Allah?" Said the disciples: "We are Allah's helpers: We believe in Allah and you bear witness that we are Muslims" (3:52).

The emphasis here is on Muslims as persons who are obedient and who submit. For another example, let us examine sura 5 aya 114,

> And behold! I inspired the Disciples to have faith in me and my apostle: They said: "We have faith, and you do bear witness that we bow to Allah as Muslims."

The Qur'an proclaims that those who obey God are Muslims—recall that *Muslim* simply means "one who submits." If a Muslim is someone who submits to God, then that is what I want to be, and I imagine you do, too. With a clear conscience I could say that I strive to be a "Muslim"—not to follow the religion of Islam, but to live my life in submission to God. That is nothing other than biblical obedience.

C. *The Place of Jesus Christ*

We have already touched on our faiths' mutual respect for Jesus. Jesus is held in great honor in the Qur'an, and even today, he is still held in great honor by Muslims. Remember, they believe in the virgin birth; they even believe in the second coming. Sura 19:19–21 describes the moment when Mary learns that she will give birth to Jesus:

> He said: "No, I am only a messenger from your Lord, [to announce] to you the gift of a holy son." She said: "How shall I have a son, since no man has touched me, and I am not unchaste?" He said: "So [it will be]: your Lord says, 'That is easy for me: And [we wish] to appoint him as a sign for men and a mercy from us': It is a matter [so] decreed."

What a surprising passage for most Christians! Similarly, sura 3:45 says,

> Behold! The angels said: "O Mary! Allah gives you glad tidings of a word from him: his name will be Christ Jesus, the son of Mary, held in honor in this world and the hereafter and of (the company of) those nearest to Allah."

Wow! And a few verses later, in verse 49, we read:

> And (appoint him) an apostle to the children of Israel (with this message): "I have come to you, with a sign from your Lord, in that I make for you out of clay, as it were, the figure of a bird, and breathe into it, and it becomes a bird by Allah's permission: And I heal those born blind, and the lepers, and I raise the dead to life, by Allah's permission; and I declare to you what you eat, and what you store in your houses." Surely therein is a sign for you, if you did believe.

Again, this passage is a clear reference to Jesus Christ. Jesus is held in honor by both the Qur'an and by Muslims. We share this connection.

About the second coming of Jesus, there are two passages most Muslims interpret to support their belief in the return of Christ.[154] What a conversation-starter!

> And there is none of the People of the Book but must believe in him before his death; and on the Day of Judgment he will be a witness against them (4:159).

> And (Jesus) shall be a Sign (for the coming of) the Hour (of Judgment): Therefore have no doubt about the (Hour), but follow Me: This is a Straight Way (43:61).

3. Use Evidences

In my outreach to Muslims, I anticipate their questions, especially in the area of the reliability of the Bible. Some Muslims really appreciate materials that clarify how the Christian Scriptures came together.[155] Other helpful areas of evidences include the problem of suffering; archaeology; and the identity of Jesus. Evidences are faith building, and are an important part of "pre-evangelism" for more and more people worldwide. That is, before we can expect others to respond to the gospel message, we must prepare the ground: pre-evangelism, then evangelism.

Every month I meet Muslims, both in the United States and abroad. Many of them have numerous questions about the Bible and basic Christian evidences. During my last visit to a Muslim country, I spent a lot of time answering a Muslim friend's questions, and I shared a good evidences book with him. We remain in touch, and I pray that our friendship will one day lead to his gaining a full appreciation of the gospel.

4. Be Prepared for the Counter-arguments

Next to consider as we build bridges with Muslims are *Islamic* evidences. Christians are not the only ones who hold public meetings defending their scriptures and answering skeptics' questions. Muslims too have long traveled the world, defending Islam, bolstering the faith of the faithful, and challenging the view of the infidel. They attempt to refute Christianity by showing that the Bible is contradictory and the Qur'an is inspired.[156]

What are the primary arguments that Muslims use either to convert people to Islam or to undermine Christianity? And how are we to respond to them?

A. *The "Miracle" of Muhammad's Literacy*

Many Muslims claim that an illiterate merchant like Muhammad could not have written the Qur'an apart from a miracle. Whether he was illiterate or not is debatable (see discussion in chapter 2). The claim is based on 7:157, where we read: "...those who shall follow the Apostle, the unlettered Prophet whom they shall find described in the Torah that is in them, and in the gospel" (7:157).

Even if Muhammad was illiterate, there are several non-miraculous explanations for how the Qur'an could have been written. Perhaps Muhammad dictated to an associate. Perhaps "unlettered" means not illiterate, but not formally educated (as in Acts 4:13—Peter and John were certainly able to write). Maybe he was less illiterate than some claim; he was, after all, a merchant, and merchants have normally achieved at least a rudimentary literacy, if for no other reason than to keep track of inventory and sales.

B. *Changed Lives*

Some say, "So many lives have been changed by Islam." The response to this is simple: Obviously, if someone believes something fervently enough, his life will begin to change—for better or worse. That is true of any religion or system. But life change does not necessarily prove that whatever inspired the change is true.

C. *Rapid Spread*

Many Muslims reason, "Islam spread so rapidly! This

proves its heavenly origin." But let us remember the religion's history. Islam spread slowly until Muhammad became successful in politics, relying on clever economic policy, backed by the sword, to promote a burgeoning religious and economic empire. Through violence, all kinds of things can spread quickly, particularly when shifting political alliances create favorable opportunities.

Still others would say, "Islam has so many converts." Indeed, it is impressive to most of us in the West that one in five human beings is a Muslim, but what does this actually prove? When you are promised paradise for converting, and the alternative is heavy taxation (or, in some cases, slavery or even death), conversion becomes an attractive option.

D. *Numerological Arguments*

Muslims commonly make other, less scholarly claims to validate their religion. For example, many say that the entire Qur'an is structured around the number 19. For example,

> Sura 1, known as the *'Basmalah,'* occupies a special position in the Qur'an... [I]t constitutes the foundation upon which the Qur'an's 19-based mathematical miracle is built. The *Basmalah* consists of 19 Arabic letters, and its constituent words (*Bism Allah Al-Rahman Al-Raheem*) occur in the Qur'an in multiples of 19: 19, 2698, 57, and 114 times, respectively. Thus, the reader is handed at the outset tangible proof that this is not a human-made book.
>
> Numerous mathematical phenomena are connected with this verse. For example, the absence of *Basmalah* from sura 9 is compensated for 19 suras later; sura 27 contains two *Basmalahs*. Thus, the count of all *Basmalahs* is restored to 114, 19x6. Additionally, when we add the sura numbers from the missing *Basmalah* (sura 27) [9+10+11+... +27], the total comes to 342, 19 x18. This total, remarkably, is also the number of words between the two *Basmalahs* of sura 27.[157]

Yet this is hardly impressive, since the same games can and have been played with Shakespeare, the Bible, and many other books. It is easy to do, provided the search parameters have been set broadly enough.

Another numerical argument is that the Arabic word for day, *yawm*, appears exactly 365 times in the Qur'an. While this is interesting, it proves little, especially since the Muslim year was not calculated by solar observation, but by *lunar* measurement. (That is, 354 days in the Islamic year.)

This is not to say that Christians have always avoided specious arguments! There are many lines of reasoning—counting the number of words in a verse, or letters in a word, etc.— which supposedly prove the inspiration of the Bible. (Or at least the inspiration of *that* version of the Bible in *that* English or other translation.) Notions of "Bible codes" have proven to be intriguing and enduring, yet they are fundamentally flawed.

E. *Embryological Cycle*

Some Muslims are fond of pointing out that the entire cycle of the development of the human embryo is found in the Qur'an. The descriptions of the embryo (from "a drop of mingled fluid" [76:2], to "a leech-like clot" [23:14], to "a chewed-like clump" [22:5; 23:14], to a being with bones and then flesh [23:14], etc.) is hailed as a clear sign from Allah.

And yet such descriptions are not unique in classical literature. In fact, the second-century physician Galen provided the same account in his medical writings.[158] Besides, no miraculous insight was required for a Muslim, or anyone else, to describe the appearance of the embryo at various stages. Miscarriages and abortions would have afforded ample opportunity.[159]

F. *The Prophet of Deuteronomy 18*

Probably the most favored Bible passage in Islamic apologetics is Deuteronomy 18:15–18. Muslims claim this text points to Muhammad:

The Lord your God will raise up for you a prophet like me from among your own brothers. You must listen to him. For this is what you asked of the Lord your God at Horeb on the day of the assembly when you said, "Let us not hear the voice of the Lord our God nor see this great fire anymore, or we will die." The Lord said to me: "What they say is good. I will raise up for them a prophet like you from among their brothers; I will put my words in his mouth, and he will tell them everything I command him."

This familiar text goes on to say that if anyone will not listen to that prophet, he will be called to account (verse 19). The speaker in the text is Moses. There was no prophet like Moses raised up by God in the Old Testament, and so when Peter speaks to the Jewish leaders, he quotes this very scripture and applies it to Jesus (Acts 3:22–26).

Which of Jesus' attributes justify Peter's claim? Jesus is like Moses in three ways: Moses led his people, he performed miracles, and he brought revelation from God to the people. Jesus also led his people. Jesus did miracles. He brought revelation from God. (His words are inspired.) No other character in the Old Testament or New Testament qualifies. This passage can *only* be talking about Jesus Christ. In fact, early Christians employed this scripture as a proof-text of Jesus' identity. In Acts 3, we see Peter using this very passage to prove that Jesus is the Messiah.

But the Muslims say that this prophecy is about Muhammad. There are several problems with that claim. First, Muhammad was not like Moses. For one thing, he did not do miracles—but there is more. Deuteronomy says that "the Lord your God will raise up for you a prophet like me from among your own brothers." If you want to check Deuteronomy 17:15 (and many other verses), you will see that a *brother* in this Jewish context refers to a fellow Jew, and never to a foreigner.

Was Muhammad a Jew? Absolutely not! To claim otherwise would be offensive to Muslims! In fact, claiming Jewish ancestry would not be a good thing for *anyone* if they parachuted into Mecca! The Scriptures show that this figure, this Messiah, would be Jewish. Jesus fits the bill, Muhammad does not.

In sura 29:27, we read a passage that sheds light on the Qur'an's understanding of the Jewish race: "We bestowed on him Isaac and Jacob, and we established the prophethood and scripture through his seed." In this passage, the pronoun *him* refers to Abraham. Abraham had two children of note: Isaac and Ishmael. Jacob was the son of Isaac, not Ishmael. Jacob had twelve sons whose descendants became the Jewish tribes. So, the Qur'an says that the prophethood and scripture are established through the seed of Jacob—that is, through the Jews—so the Qur'an knows the difference between the Jews and others.

By the way, nowhere does the Qur'an say that Deuteronomy 18 is referring to Muhammad, but even so, it is a popular text used in Islamic evidences.

G. *Deuteronomy 33 and Other Passages*

Deuteronomy 33:1–2 is also employed by Islamic apologists:

> This is the blessing that Moses the man of God pronounced on the Israelites before his death. He said: "The Lord came from Sinai and dawned over them from Seir; he shone forth from Mount Paran. He came with myriads of holy ones from the south, from his mountain slopes."

Some Muslim apologists claim that in this passage, Sinai refers to Moses, Seir refers to Jesus, and Paran refers to Muhammad. They appear to be assuming that Paran is in Arabia, which is unlikely. But regardless of its location, Seir was the home of the Edomites, and has nothing to do with Jesus. To try to say that this verse refers to Muhammad is just astounding. It is a real stretch.

Muslims claim Muhammad is even greater the Moses. Yet Deuteronomy 34:10–11 says, "Since then, no prophet has risen in Israel like Moses, whom the Lord knew face to face, who did all those miraculous signs and wonders." If Muhammad was really a prophet greater than Moses, is it not reasonable to expect that he too would have worked miracles? But one cannot apply this passage to Muhammad, because he *never* performed miracles.

Habakkuk 3:3 reads, "God came from Teman, the Holy One from Mount Paran." Once again, Muslims claim that the Holy One from Paran is Muhammad, but Paran is nowhere near Mecca.[160] Muhammad was from Medina and Mecca.

Several other Old Testament passages are enlisted in support of Muslim claims. In Psalm 45:3–5, we find what the Muslims say is a description of Muhammad as the prophet of the sword. Verse 4 reads, "Gird your sword upon your side, O mighty one; clothe yourself with splendor and majesty." The problem with applying this to Muhammad is that verse 6 of Psalm 45 goes on to say that this figure will be *God*, and that is why Hebrews 1 quotes Psalm 45 as a reference to Jesus. No Muslim would say, "Oh, yes, Muhammad is God." That would be anathema.

Finally, in Isaiah 21:7, we read about chariots and riders on donkeys and camels. According to Muslim apologists, the chariots refer to Jesus and Muhammad. Yet this passage is talking about the fall of Babylon. It has nothing to do with Jesus, and certainly has nothing to do with Muhammad.

None of the Old Testament passages mustered in support of Muhammad say what they are claimed to teach.

H. *John the Baptist's Prophecy*

In Matthew 3:11, John the Baptist says, "But after me will come one more powerful than I, whose sandals I am not fit to carry." Muslims say that the one who is coming is Muhammad. Yet that assertion simply does not work. Muhammad does not baptize people into fire and spirit, as John says. Nor is Muhammad the one that the New Testament points to as John's successor, the one for whom John the Baptist paved the way. The Bible makes it clear that John the Baptist was preparing people's hearts to receive the message of Jesus.

I. John 14

One of Muslims' most incredible claims is that John 14:16 prophesies Muhammad. Now, to appreciate what the Muslims have done here, you should know that Muhammad means "the praised one," or "he is praised." In John 14:16–17, we read, "And I will ask the Father, and he will give you another Counselor to be with you forever—the Spirit of truth." Some versions say that God would send an advocate, or a paraclete. The passage is clearly referring to the Holy Spirit. The Greek word translated "counselor" is *parakletos.*

Some Muslim apologists even affirm that the original word was *periclytos,* which means "the praised one" (a common epithet of Muhammad, as in 61:6). This claim is completely unsupported by the manuscript evidence. Many ancient manuscripts of John have survived, and none of them has *periclytos* in place of *parakletos.* Remember, Jesus said, "I will send you another Counselor in my name." Without any manuscript support, one can make all kinds of wild claims. But you don't even have to explore all the ancient manuscripts to rebut the Muslim claim! If you look ten verses later, in verse 26, you see that Jesus explicitly identifies the helper or counselor as the Holy Spirit. All you have to do to learn the truth is hang with the passage and look at the context. Jesus is not talking about a person, and he certainly is not talking about Muhammad.

If you need further proof, in John 16 Jesus tells us that this helper will abide *forever.* He will remain forever—but Muhammad died. In John 14:26, we learn that this helper, the counselor, would be sent *in Jesus' name,* but no Muslim would allow that Muhammad came "in the name of Jesus"! Further-more, in Acts 1:5, Jesus says that the counselor would come soon—in a few days—not in the seventh century. Six hundred years is hardly "soon."

J. No One Can Pay for the Sins of Another

Muslims say that one reason they cannot fully embrace Christianity is because no one can atone for someone else's sins, only for his own. They have a serious problem with the concept of Jesus as the atoning sacrifice for mankind's sin. Ezekiel 18:20 is commonly cited: "The person who sins shall die. A child shall not suffer for the iniquity of a parent, nor a parent suffer for the iniquity of a child; the righteousness of the righteous shall be his own, and the wickedness of the wicked shall be his own."

But in fact, the concept of substitutionary atonement is not absent from Islam. For one, Muslims believe that Ishmael's death was averted by the death of a ram, following the ac-count in Genesis 22 (yet substituting Ishmael for Isaac). At the Feast of *'Id al-Fitr*, a goat is slain for the purification of the faithful. Moreover, the Shi'ites describe Muhammad's grand-son Husayn, who was murdered, as a "ransom for the people, for Mankind."[161]

Even so, the notion that Jesus would be crucified is re-jected by Muslims out of hand; they claim that all God's proph-ets proved their truthfulness through divine protection and success in their life's work. And, as in Judaism, Islam finds abominable the idea that Jesus, an innocent man, would be "murdered" by God for sins he did not commit. The crucifixion is disparaged as "human sacrifice."

Yet this is hardly a fair criticism of Christianity. Christ *willingly* went to his death, so no murder is involved on the part of God. Had Jesus not been perfectly sinless—a fact Muslims acknowledge—he could not have borne our sins. Psalm 49:7-9 says, "No *man* can redeem the life of another or give to God a ransom for him—the ransom for a life is costly, no payment is ever enough—that he should live on forever and not see decay." And yet Jesus was no mere *man*. Were he a sinner, like us, certainly the Muslims would be right: He could not have borne our sins. Nor was the sacrifice to appease an angry deity; rather, the Cross is an expression of God's infinite love (Romans 5:1–11).

A further point to be made is this: In bearing our sin, Christ actually ceased to be innocent! He took our sin on himself. 2 Corinthians 5:21 says, "God made him who had no sin to be sin for us, so that in him we might become God's righteousness." So Jesus was *not* the innocent dying for the guilty. Because of our sin, he was actually the *guilty* dying for the guilty!

Such is the scandal of the cross (1 Corinthians 1:18ff). The crucified Christ is a stumbling block to Jews (and Muslims), and foolishness to Gentiles.

4. Anticipate!

In short, although the standard Muslim arguments used in trying to convert Christians are invalid, being familiar with them enables us to interact with a lower level of anxiety. Confidence, when forced or faked, does not fool many people. In evangelistic outreach, our confidence comes from the Lord. But it also comes from competence (knowing our stuff). The combination of *competence* and *confidence* greatly enhances our *credibility*.

No passage in Scripture refers to Muhammad. In fact, if any passages indirectly refer to Muhammad, they do so only to *forbid* us to follow him! In Galatians 1:8, Paul says, "But even if we or an angel from heaven should preach a gospel other than the one we preached to you, let him be eternally condemned," or let him be anathema. No one will be saved who perverts the gospel and teaches another gospel, even if they heard it from an angel in heaven. A similar passage is 1 Kings 13, where the young prophet forfeits his life because he believes an older prophet who claims to have a message from an angel. The old prophet claims that an angel spoke to him, the young prophet falls for the lie, and God does not spare him. The young prophet is killed by a lion.

The Bible is clear that the gospel has been once for all delivered (Jude 3). Even if someone were contacted by an angel, as Muhammad claims to have been, we should not listen to him.

5. Explain Key Christian Concepts

Certain Christian concepts are especially difficult for Muslims to grasp or embrace. If we are to be effective in sharing our faith, we must learn to amend or counter any misinformation or misunderstanding they may have, and to explain the Christian view in a way that makes sense to a Muslim.

A. The Son of God

The Qur'an repeatedly avers that Allah has no consorts or sons. A consort goddess would be a female companion of Allah—something unthinkable to a Muslim. In ancient Arabian religion, there were many gods and consort goddesses. Let us recall that in the original Qur'an Allah had several daughters, just like the ancient Greek and Roman gods we read about in school. The Greek, Roman, and Arabian gods had affairs, married (or had liaisons), and procreated. They were sexual beings, yet in the Qur'an, Allah possesses no sexuality. Allah is a male figure, but he has no wife; there is no sex.

O People of the Book, exceed not the limits of your religion nor speak anything about Allah, but the truth. The Messiah, Jesus, son of Mary, is only a messenger of Allah and His word which He communicated to Mary and a mercy from Him. So believe in Allah and His messengers. And say not, *Three*. Desist, it is better for you. Allah is only one God. Far be it from His glory to have a son (sura 4:171).

Seventh-century Muslims seem to have thought that Christians believed that God had a wife and children. In the Middles Ages, when the Qur'an was written, Christians spoke of Jesus and Mary in quite physical ways. They referred to Mary as the mother of God.[162] In the mind of Muhammad, Jesus being God's son must have implied that there was a time when Jesus was *not* God's son—which in turn implied that God had procreated in a physical sense. That is not what the Bible teaches, but that is what many people thought, including some sects of Christians.

To a Muslim, who believes that Allah has no consorts or sons, this teaching is a serious problem: To say that Jesus is the son of God implies that Jesus is not eternal, and that he is God's physical son. How can we answer Muslims on this point?

Part of the solution lies in choosing the right word when we describe Jesus as God's son. The point about sonship is countered easily by distinguishing between the Arabic words *ibn* and *walad*. In Arabic, one word for *son* is *ibn*. You see that word all the time, and it is often used in a figurative sense. There is another word, though, for a son, or for a child or offspring: *walad*. Walad suggests that there has been conception and pregnancy. That is not the word that we would use, of course, when talking about Jesus as God's son in Arabic. We would use the word *ibn*.

Some Islamic countries use colloquial phrases like *"ibn-ussabil." "Ibn-ussabil"* means "the son of the road." A traveler who is on the road all the time would be called "a son of the road." That does not mean that the road is his father or mother; it's just an expression. In the Hebrew Old Testament we come across the phrase, "the son of the prophets." If you study the Old Testament, you know that the phrase does not mean that the person's father was literally a prophet. "Son of the prophets" means that he is a member of the group of prophets, the guild of prophets—regardless of his father or mother's occupation! Similarly, in English you might describe a fiery or colorful person as "a son of a gun." The epithet does not mean that one of his parents was a pistol or a rifle. The point is that there are figurative ways of understanding the word *son.*

In the same way, Jesus is not literally God's son, in the sense that there was a time when he was not God's son, and then God, through sexual relations, became a father. Not at all. In Christianity the word *son* refers to the relationship—not in time, but in nature—the *personal* nature of the relationship. Jesus is and has always been God's son.

To illustrate, we might say, "The tree is in the field." That statement implies, I think, that at one time the field had no tree growing in it—one day, a seed sprouted and the tree began to grow in the field. But this is not necessarily so. Perhaps the field used to be a wood, and only one tree survived. In that case, the tree might be older than the field!

To continue our analogy, the tree and field could have come into existence at the same time. The field could have been a rocky moraine, gradually changing into a field as sediment accumulated and grasses grew during the same time that the tree was growing. So whereas normally we would assume that one thing always precedes the other, this is not necessarily the case. This explains how Jesus can be God's son without being younger than the Father.

But even if you convince a Muslim that, in theory, Jesus could be God's son, the argument might not end there. Muslims would say that God could not become a man. To a Muslim, the incarnation of Jesus is impossible. Yet Muslims believe that flesh and spirit unite in a human being, so why could not God and man unite in one human body? If we appeal to a fact that Muslims already accept, and then adapt it in a Christological direction, the incarnation starts to become more understandable.

Notice also that in Q 4:171 Jesus is Allah's "Word." Given the connection with John 1:1,14,18, this passage still has a high view of Jesus, even if we agreed with the Muslims that Jesus isn't the Son of God.

B. *The Trinity*

Muhammad's rejection of the Trinity was a reaction against seventh-century Catholic Christianity. His critique of Christianity was partly correct, but what he criticized were doctrines and practices not supported by the New Testament. In fact, Muhammad agreed with the Bible's teachings on many subjects, at least the parts he was familiar with.

Yet even in Islam there is a sort of "trinity." Muslims believe that Allah, the Spirit of Allah, and the word of Allah are all eternal. This is the "Muslim trinity."

C. *The Eternity of Christ*

We must also prepare to explain the eternity of Christ. Muslims claim that Jesus cannot be eternal—in the sense of being everlasting, existing infinitely in time in both directions. Christians believe that God is eternal and God's Word is eternal. The Bible says so in the Psalms, in Matthew, and in many other places—but Christians also believe that Jesus is eternal.[163] And yet Muslims *already* believe in two eternal and uncreated entities: Allah and the Qur'an.[164] So Muslims believe in two eternal, uncreated entities. Christians believe in three— here we are not that far apart in our beliefs! In explaining this concept, we can draw upon our related beliefs.

6. *Appreciate the Strengths of Muslims*

We cannot win over our Muslim friends if we do not acknowledge their strengths with respect and appreciation. Many Muslims behave more righteously than those who claim to be Christians. Did you know that most Muslims tend to drink less alcohol and live more moral lives than so-called Christians? Muslims, as a whole, are far less promiscuous than Christians. Many Muslims will not watch immoral television programs or movies—and yet many "Christians" watch these programs without a second thought. I offer these examples to our shame.

During the Crusades, the Muslims tended to be more merciful than the Christians. The idea behind the Crusades was that the Christians would take the Holy Land back from the Muslims. The Christians reasoned, "Possession of the Holy Land is our divine right; we should take it back." The Crusades represent a time of great ugliness and shameful treatment of Muslims. The abuse went both ways, but it is often more embarrassing to read about what the so-called Christians did.

At times, Muslims have risen above the divisive in-fighting that can dominate Christian denominations. In Jerusalem, the Church of the Holy Sepulchre is said to stand over the place where Jesus was crucified, buried, and resurrected. This church, which was built in the fourth century, is fiercely guarded and controlled by six different Christian denominations: Roman Catholic, Greek Orthodox, Armenian Apostolic, Ethiopian Orthodox, Coptic Orthodox, and Syrian Orthodox. In fact, these factions have fought throughout history, sometimes in actual fistfights. What a testimony to the unity of Christians!

You might wonder who retains the key to the Church of the Holy Sepulchre. For many generations, because the Christian groups have been suspicious of each other, the key has been entrusted to two Muslim families. The Muslims are the arbitrators, and are respected because they remain above the fray.

Why am I saying these things? Are we Christians afraid to "give away points"? Are we afraid to admit the shameful parts of our own legacy? If a Muslim points out the disunity of Christians or the anti-Christian behavior during the Crusades, we can respond in several ways. If a Muslim points out the disunity of Christians, or the anti-Christian behavior during the Crusades, we can respond in several ways: we can ignore the accusations; we can attempt to defend our mistakes; or we can own them.

By owning them, I do not mean that Christians must say, "Yes, those were definitely true Christians, and yes, the Bible is kind of difficult to understand." We might say, "Yes, people who claimed to be Christians did those things, and they were wrong, and if I lived back then, I hope I would not have gone that way." But how do we know what we would have done?

Perhaps it is best just to say that what those people did was not in accord with what Jesus taught. They did wrong. They did not do wrong by following what Jesus taught; they did wrong because they *ignored* what Jesus taught. That kind of humble response is not only righteous and fair, but may even open up an avenue for dialogue.

7. Read the Qur'an

Let me revisit another point I have made throughout the book: If you want to share your faith with a Muslim, it is essential that you read the Bible *and* the Qur'an. Why do I keep saying this? Because when you discuss Christianity with a Muslim, at some point, you will ask if they have read the Bible. They may have read parts, but imagine if they asked *you*, "Have you read the whole Bible, Christian?" If you answer, "No," or "Not all of it," then you have already undermined your own arguments! You want to be familiar with the whole Bible. Read it, and read it often. Then you have credibility, and perhaps even the high ground.

Strategies for Connecting with Muslims

- Study the Qur'an.
- Read books about Islam.
- Follow current events in the news.
- Become culturally aware.
- Engage on a personal level.

But you will gain even more credibility if you can say, "I have read the whole Bible, but I have also read the whole Qur'an. Have you read the Qur'an?" Most Muslims will answer, "Well, no, I have only read parts, but not as much as I would like to." Do you understand the leverage you would have in a discussion, the positive impression you would make, if you have read the whole Qur'an once or twice? I will say it again: Read the Qur'an and take notes.

You can also educate yourself by going beyond the Qur'an and reading books about Islam. Familiarize yourself with works on Muhammad and Muslims, on *jihad* and militant Islam, on Israel and the Palestinian question. As noted earlier, my favorite book is by Geisler and Saleeb, called *Answering Islam*.[165] There are also many informative websites. For suggestions, consult the Appendix: Resources for Further Study, for more than a hundred recommended books and websites.

8. Aim to Become Politically Aware

Next, aim to become politically aware. I am not advocating that Christians should engage in politics. The early church seems to have avoided politics completely, as did Jesus. Yet at the very least we can:

- Read the newspaper. Keep an eye on foreign affairs. Don't jump directly to sports, fashion, the comics, or whatever your favorite section is. Aim to become aware of what is happening in the world around us—the world that is one-fifth Muslim!
- Watch the news. But of course, be wary of the fear-mongers, those who want to control you by preying upon your fear. We are not to fear man. As Psalm 27 reminds us, "The Lord is our light." He is the reason we are confident. But that does not mean that we should ignore what is going on in our world. You do not even have to read a newspaper. You could read the news online or watch news broadcasts. But the important thing is that we understand what is going on around us.
- Push yourself to experience different cultures. Sample the cuisines of foreign lands. When reaching out to someone from another country, learn a few words and phrases from his or her country. Read a little about the history of your Muslim friend's country of origin.

- Pray for all the world. Internalize Jesus' global vision for evangelism: "Go and make disciples of all nations…" (Matthew 28:19). We must not retreat into the cultural cocoons of our entertainment-oriented society. Christians are called to "go."

9. Challenge the Dominant Cultural Myth

Awareness will help us to avoid silly discussions and foolish quarrels, and it will also help us to show our Muslim friends that we care and are different. Evangelistic Christians are not like the unthinking masses. No, we truly care about others—all people—and we are willing to take some steps to meet them. This does not mean meeting halfway in an ill-conceived, ecumenical compromise of doctrine and faith, but meeting them emotionally in a place of understanding. We need to be people of compassion *and* conviction.

In the first chapter, we considered the popular myth that all roads lead to the top of the mountain—that all roads lead to God. We have to question that myth—one that is easily disproven. To speak and act with integrity, we need to be men and women with sufficient conviction not to fall for popular ideas. We cannot convert anyone—nor can we please God!—if we do not address this politically correct concept in a straightforward and biblical manner.

10. Engage on a Personal Level

It goes without saying that we are not likely to win Muslims for Christ if we are not building relationships with any. How many Muslims have you reached out to this year? We need to engage on a personal level with Muslims. The purpose of this book is not just to inform us. The challenge issued by this book is not just to get to know the Qur'an and learn some history, or the appeal to embrace a different way of thinking. No, the Muslim challenge is the call to do all that and, even more importantly, to reach out to Muslims; to care, to show

God's love in this world; to be light and salt, to be Jesus to the world.

As this book draws to a close, I would like to share a letter from a Muslim seeker. When I first read these words, they moved me deeply. It was a letter to the editor published in *Christianity Today* in December, 2001. As I recall, shortly before this letter was written, armed militants had burst into a church in Pakistan and a horrible massacre ensued. The Muslim terrorists slaughtered the worshipers mercilessly—men, women, children. This event had a profound effect upon the Muslim who wrote this letter. He opens his heart to us as he ponders the possible reactions of American Christians, to whom he fears he represents what is bad in Islam.

Dear Mr. Yancey,

Considering the terrible tragedy that happened yesterday in this nation... I think I should write this letter, because I am convinced now that evil does exist in this world.

Growing up in Pakistan, I was a moderately religious Muslim. During the past few months, some of the [painful] events in my life caused me to think about God... I read some books about the prophet Muhammad and the Islamic faith by Western scholars. I was shocked to learn a lot of things about my religion that I never knew. I felt—and still feel—betrayed and hurt. In a closed society like Pakistan, any sort of criticism of Islam is punishable by death, so one cannot have an unbiased view of the faith.

For [me as] a Muslim person to be that interested in the Christian faith is unthinkable. [My family and I] have talked about issues like the concept of salvation in Islam (which is through deeds) and that of Christianity. They find it quite ridiculous—the concept of a Savior and one person dying for everyone's sins, and that all you have to do is to believe in him. To be honest, I find this concept a little strange too... [yet] I found myself defending the Christian beliefs against my family, arguing that the Crucifixion is a historical fact and that someone who is so special as to be born of a virgin [as the Qur'an teaches]—and who would even come back to the world [also a Qur'anic teaching]—can't be just a prophet of God.

But the most painful discovery for me about the Islamic faith has been its concept of militancy. I always used to think that these fanatics were just misguided people who give Islam a bad name. To be sure, Islam does not permit killing of innocent women and children, but as I have found out, its teachings are quite different from those of Jesus, who wants you to turn the other cheek. As I know now, violence does have a strong precedent in Islam.

The terrible tragedy that happened yesterday in this country seems to be the logical outcome of teachings that tell you it's okay to reply in kind. I think that's what happens when you try to enforce God's will in this earthly world rather than believing that his kingdom is not of this world, but of the other world...

I know that if I decide to convert, I will be causing an immense amount of heartbreak. I would be ostracized by all my relatives. Also, my legal status in this country expires next year, and considering my views about Islam now... I can't imagine going back to Pakistan.

Do you think I would find loving and open-minded friends in the church? Would it be fair to say some people would put their guards up and won't want anything to do with someone who belongs to some different, Asian Indian race? Someone who has a different color of skin and speaks with an accent?

I really am so confused, so lost. Please tell me what to do. God bless you.[166]

Does that stir your emotions, as it did mine? This man has become convinced of the truths of Christianity, but has not yet been convinced of the truth of the love of Christians. I wonder how many more Muslim seekers there are in the world, searching for answers and for God, who need to see the love of Christ put into action.

And that, ultimately, is the purpose of this book. It is my hope that, while you have gleaned information about facts and dates and doctrine, you have also gained something far more valuable. I hope that you have attained a sense of understanding and conviction that spurs you on. I hope you will continue to prepare and educate yourself, not simply for education's sake, but for the sake of love.

Make it your ambition to be ready, so that as you have the opportunity, you may love and share with any Muslim you encounter. The apostle Peter urges us:

> "Always be prepared to give an answer to everyone who asks you to give the reason for the hope that you have. But do this with gentleness and respect, keeping a clear conscience, so that those who speak maliciously against your good behavior in Christ may be ashamed of their slander" (1 Peter 3:15–16).

As we strive to connect with Muslims, let us view them as fellow human beings, not as demons or merely targets of conversion. (Not that we do not want them to respond to the gospel, of course—but we should love them even if they are not interested in becoming Christians.)

We can be peacemakers who help to heal the centuries of troubled relationships between those living under the Cross and those under the Crescent. But first we must open our minds, our hearts, our Bibles and our Qur'ans.

Jesus & Muslims
Will We Follow Our Lord?

"And who is my neighbor?"

—Luke 10:29b

Reading this book, do you feel as if you are swimming in a sea of information? Particularly if you haven't already been familiar with Islam, you may find that the information and admonishments I have presented are almost overwhelming. But take heart! Simply by taking the time to read this book, you have shown integrity and compassion—a willingness to explore a new religion and culture—rather than sitting around, complacent in your old assumptions and prejudices. Coming to understand a different religion, culture and way of thinking is a daunting task, one that cannot be accomplished in a few weeks or even months of study—but every effort that we make to educate ourselves is a step in the right direction!

I encourage you to continue educating yourself not only about Islam, but about other religions and cultures as well. After all, the Bible exhorts us; "And the Lord's servant must not quarrel; instead, he must be kind to everyone, able to teach, not resentful. Those who oppose him he must gently instruct, in the hope that God will grant them repentance leading them to a knowledge of the truth, and that they will come to their senses and escape from the trap of the devil, who has taken them captive to do his will" (2 Timothy 2:24–26). If we are to "gently instruct" others, we must continually add to our own knowledge, so that we may be equipped to answer their questions. Once again, as 1 Peter 3:15–16 teaches, "Always be prepared to give an answer... with gentleness and respect, keeping a clear conscience."

By reading *Jesus and Islam,* you have taken a great first step toward better understanding Islam and its followers. But now that you have some knowledge, what should you do with the understanding you have gained? I urge you to take your education out of the theoretical realm, and begin using it in your daily life and interactions. How do you accomplish such a feat? It is in that question that we come to the heart of the issue, the whole point of our study.

A picture is worth a thousand words. Jesus made few doctrinal pronouncements. The primary way he taught his followers was through his own personal example. Thankfully, his life provides us with a wonderful example of how to interact with differing cultures and religions. So rather than wondering, "How should I relate to the 1.4 billion Muslims of the world?" it would be more fruitful to ask, in the well-known words of Charles Sheldon, "What would Jesus do?" Fortunately, the gospels give us an *excellent* idea of how the Lord would have approached Muslims.

The Samaritans

It so happens that there was a misunderstood and much-maligned group in Jesus' day that has a number of things in common with the Muslims. The parallel between the Samaritans and the Jews, on the one hand, and the Muslims and the rest of the world, on the other, is apt.

The Samaritans came into existence in the eighth century BC during the traumatic time when the northern kingdom of Israel finally capitulated to the Neo-Assyrian Empire. The result of intermarriage and religious eclecticism, the Samaritans were despised by the Jews (Judeans, the inhabitants of the southern kingdom of Judah who were able to avoid decimation) as racial half-breeds. Moreover, with their own (altered) version of the Torah,[167] the Samaritans were not kosher. They were heterodox, not orthodox, having rewritten the Bible for their own purposes. You can read about their origins in 2 Kings 17.

The Samaritans were not only denigrated,[168] but completely avoided as unclean.[169] Centuries of antipathy and misunderstanding had led to a polarized and seemingly intractable situation. In the New Testament, the tension between Jews and Samaritans is palpable.[170]

Similarly, Muslims are different from Jews and Christians, both ethnically and religiously. Claiming common descent from Abraham, along with the Jews, they were rejected as Abraham's children nonetheless. And as we have seen, they have rewritten the word of God for their own purposes. More often than not, especially in the West, followers of Islam are looked at askance. This is not to say that their doctrine is correct or that they have a saving faith. But whatever their error and sins, they are still God's children, at least in the most general sense (Acts 17:28), and we should love them as we love ourselves.

What did Jesus do? For the way he treated the Samaritans is, I believe, the way he would treat Muslims today.

1. Jesus ate with them.

Jesus was criticized for being a friend of "sinners" (Matthew 9:11; Mark 2:16; Luke 5:30). Yet he ate with

sinners, extending the love of God through his personal
outreach, regardless of the criticisms heaped upon him as
a result. In the same way, Jesus shared fellowship with
the Samaritans (John 4:40).

Ask yourself, "When was the last time I shared a meal
with a Muslim? Have I befriended any follower of Islam?"
Yes, the bigots may berate you: "What are you doing, eating with terrorists?" But the real question is, Are you willing to follow your Lord?

2. He emphasized the good, not the bad.

Luke 17 is an amazing chapter, and its most remark-
able section may well be the account of the healing of the
ten lepers (verses 12–19). Why did the Holy Spirit select
this event for inclusion in the gospel? Especially since the
only one to return and give thanks for his healing was
a Samaritan? Probably for the same reason that Jesus
drew attention to this man: "Was no one found to return
and give praise to God except this foreigner [a Samari-
tan]?" (v.18). In so doing, Jesus simultaneously exposed
the Jews' prejudices and drew attention to a Samaritan's
positive qualities.

Are we looking for dirt, for reasons to distance ourselves from Islam *and from Muslims?* If so, we are not imi-
tating our Lord. We are overlooking the goodness and po-
tential in our fellow human beings. We are seeing them as
objects.

Do we look for the good in others, or the bad? When
we mention other religions, do we accentuate the base,
or seek the excellent? Would we be content for others to
judge our religion only by its worst exemplars? Of course
not! When we compare Islam to Christianity, let's remember to compare the *best* of Islam to the best of Christianity, and so forth.

3. Jesus exposed prejudice.

Jesus Christ made the hated Samaritans the heroes of

his stories, and so I believe he would do with the Muslims, were he ministering on the earth today. Allow me the liberty to retool the Parable of the Good Samaritan for a Western audience, attempting to faithfully update it in its biblical context (Luke 10:25–37).

On one occasion a Western evangelical Christian, versed in the Scriptures, stood up to test Jesus. "Teacher," he asked, "what must I do to inherit eternal life?"

"What is written in the Bible?" he replied. "How do you read it?"

He answered: "'Love the Lord your God with all your heart and with all your soul and with all your strength and with all your mind; and, 'Love your neighbor as yourself.'"

"You have answered correctly," Jesus replied. "Do this and you will live."

But he wanted to justify himself, so he asked Jesus, "And just who is my neighbor?"

In reply Jesus said: "One night a man was driving down from New York to Washington, D.C., when his engine overheated. Standing by the highway as he reached for his cell phone, he was jumped by thugs on motorcycles. They robbed him, took his valuables, and beat him, leaving him by the road, bleeding.

"A Catholic happened to be driving right past him, but when he saw the man, he pulled into the far lane and kept on driving.

"So too, a Protestant, when he came to the place and saw him, drove around the body and kept going.

"Then a Muslim, when he saw the robbery victim, came where the man was; and when he got out of his car and saw him, took pity on him.

"He went to him and bandaged his wounds—for he knew some first aid—and gave him a drink of water. Then he helped the man into his car, and drove him to a motel, watching over him all night.

"The next day he gave two hundred dollars to the manager. 'Please look after him,' he said, 'and when I return, I'll reimburse you for any extra expense you may have.'

"Which of these three do you think was a neighbor to the man who was beaten and robbed?"

The Bible believer replied, "The one who had mercy on him."

Jesus told him, "Go and do likewise."

—Luke 10:25–37, *modernized*

The point isn't so much that "even" Muslims can be good people, as that we all should show brotherly love to our fellow man. *Everyone* is our neighbor, not just the person from our own "tribe." Just as the original (Jewish) audience would have taken offense at Jesus' making the Samaritan the hero—thus exposing their own prejudice and lack of love—likewise, hearers of the modernized version of the parable would be *caught* in their bias and lack of love.[171] When we are shocked by the virtue and humaneness of the Muslim, we expose our own narrow-mindedness. The parable provides a glimpse in the mirror—a view into the darkness of our own hearts.

As the light goes on—in this moment of recognition—it is up to the hearer either to change or to slip back into the common mentality of the day, with all its unjustified prejudices. We, too, can use anecdotes and illustrations to open the minds of the prejudiced.

4. He engaged in personal conversation.

Jesus interacted at a personal level with the Samaritan woman (John 4:7ff). You will notice that in this account he discussed not only her faith, but also her life (1 Thessalonians 2:8). For this she was grateful. The result: An entire community came to understand the truth in Christ (John 4:42).

I have had opportunities to meet numerous Muslims—to talk with them, share my life with them, and enjoy meals together. In 2008 I had my first debate with a Muslim. My opponent was Shabir Ally, one of the Muslim world's foremost apologists.[170] He is a real person, not an abstract stereotype of a Muslim. When we first met, he gave me a gift, telling me that he hoped this would be the beginning of a genuine friendship. The debate was cordial—serious, but not *too* serious. The following day, we had breakfast together, talking freely about issues in Christianity and Islam. And we continue to be in contact. What people most often notice when they watch these debates is the respectful dialogue. (And no, I am not ceding my position or compromising the truth of the gospel.) They can't help noticing the warmth and respect we show each other, even when we are disagreeing about matters of life and death.

How can we have passion for the truth *and* love for the one resisting the truth? See 2 Timothy 2:23–26 for the Apostle Paul's advice in this matter.

5. He challenged them to know and obey Scripture.

In Jesus' conversation with the Samarian woman, he called her to obey the scriptures (John 4:18, 22). Similarly, in his interaction with the leper, he told him to obey the law (Luke 17:14; Leviticus 14:2).

In the same way, we need to introduce Muslims to the Bible—both Old Testament and New Testament—to which, after all, their Qur'an constantly refers. Encourage them to read the Bible, and urge them to pray, asking God, "Show me the truth." Do we not think he will (Matthew 7:8)?

6. He rebuked those who advocated violence.

When Jesus' own apostles counseled violence against the Samaritans, Jesus was firmly opposed to this ungodly course of action.

> And he sent messengers ahead of him, who went and entered a village of the Samaritans, to make ready for him; but the people would not receive him, because his face was set toward Jerusalem. And when his disciples James and John saw it, they said, "Lord, do you want us to bid fire come down from heaven and consume them?" But he turned and rebuked them. And they went on to another village (Luke 9:52–55).

It was not only the Jews who were prejudiced against the Samaritans. It went both ways. In this episode, as Jesus is making his way to Jerusalem to make his final stand (and die), he was rejected by Samaritan villagers because of his destination. In a sense it wasn't personal; they weren't rejecting *him* so much as what they thought he stood for.

James and John, two of his foremost followers, suggested incineration as a suitable consequence for the Samaritans' lack of openness.[172] Jesus *rebuked* them. He understood that there was always another village. Not everyone is closed-minded. (And even those who are may well change in time, especially if we don't reply in kind.)

Violence is not the way of Christ. The Qur'an allows retaliation,[173] but Jesus never did. He would have had none of it!

7. He viewed them as real people, not stereotypes.

All told, Jesus viewed the suspect and outcast Samaritans—who, as we have seen, in several respects resemble the Muslims—*as real people*. He refused to objectify them; he rejected the stereotypes.

I am reminded of my family's next-door neighbors during my teenage years. I was bothered by my parents' disdain for our Iranian neighbors. They scorned them, making disparaging comments—mainly because they did not keep their lawn properly mowed! They were "dirty." At the time my mother was seriously considering becoming a Christian. And at that time, the Iranians were receiving a lot of bad press.

I showed my mother Matthew 6:15, where Jesus says, "For if you forgive others their trespasses, your heavenly Father will also forgive you; but if you do not forgive others, neither will your Father forgive your trespasses" (RSV). I said to my mother, "If you're prejudiced against your neighbor, you cannot become a real Christian." I also showed her 1 John 4:20, which reads, "Those who say, 'I love God,' and hate their brothers or sisters, are liars; for those who do not love a brother or sister whom they have seen, cannot love God whom they have not seen." The point was not wasted. My mother walked next door to meet the neighbors, bringing them a meal and inviting the woman to a Bible study. Soon after, my mother gave her life to Christ in repentance and baptism.

Romans 12:2 tells us we cannot, must not, think the way the world thinks. "Do not be conformed to this world, but be transformed by the renewing of your minds, so that you may discern what is the will of God—what is good and acceptable and perfect." When we allow prejudice to govern our attitudes and actions, we are in direct violation of Scripture.

Much of the religious world is steeped in prejudice. That makes it all the more important that true Christians follow the Lord. Like you and me, Muslims have hearts of flesh; dreams and disappointments; fears and hopes. As we have said, the Bible instructs us to "always be prepared to give an answer to everyone who asks you to give the reason for the hope you have" (1 Peter 3:15). We are called to know what we are talking about. Moreover, we are to share our faith "with gentleness and respect" (1 Peter 3:16). It doesn't matter what socioeconomic, racial, political, or religious group the outsider belongs to. This means our Muslim friends are no exception.

A few questions to ask yourself as we conclude our study:

- Is my attitude towards Muslims radically different from that of those around me? Have I been affected by the media or by popular prejudices, harboring a negative view of Muslims?
- Do I respect followers of Muhammad? And do I have enough of a love for them to be gentle in my approach?
- Am I prepared to explain my faith? Do I know not only the Qur'an but (especially) the Bible well enough to engage in intelligent discussion about religion?

Once we reject stereotypical thinking, genuine connection becomes possible.

Summary

Although you have reached the end of this book, you may still have numerous questions about Islam and Muslims. I have not attempted to provide an exhaustive education into Islam and the Qur'an, or into Arab culture. My aim has been to introduce you to a fundamental understanding and to open your eyes, your mind, and your heart to a broader way of thinking and a deeper love for your fellow man. And while I encourage you to continue adding to your knowledge, at this juncture only one question is important: *Am I willing to reach out as Jesus did, without favoritism or prejudice? Am I ready to continue to learn about Islam, extending an open hand of fellowship to Muslims in a peaceable and loving spirit?*

If we are prepared to follow the Lord in his gracious spirit of outreach, renouncing violence, hate, and prejudice, we will become part of the solution, not the problem. Together let us take the high road, allowing the Spirit of Christ to work and speak through us. Let us take the light to the Muslim world!

Postscript:
A Personal Reflection
by Abdel Aziz Sarah

From Theory to Practice: A Case Study in Muslim Conversion

I am the typical Arab male: dark brown skin, large full eyebrows, and a heavy beard. I speak loudly and use hand gestures when I talk. To many Americans my appearance is equated with fear and the unknown. But I am a Christian. My Muslim name is Abdel Aziz, which means "Servant of (God) the Great," and I grew up in Jerusalem in a world foreign to most of you.

I was raised Muslim, the youngest of seven children. As a child I attended the Al-Aqsa School, which focused on teaching the Islamic way of life. We had daily classes on Islam, where we learned how to read and interpret the Qur'an and Hadith. I started attending the mosque when I was five years old, and prayed to Allah five times a day. From the age of six, I fasted during the month of Ramadan (no food or water from sunrise to sunset). By the time I was seven years old, I had memorized all the key verses in the Qur'an, and learned how to lead prayers.

I even called the faithful to prayer in the mosque! I was a good Muslim boy, by all definitions. My family was very proud of me. My father would wake up at 4:30 a.m. to accompany me to the mosque, and the women in my family wore the veil.

Growing up, I had plenty of exposure to Christianity as well. Jerusalem is a city of religion, and I was raised in a center of Christian and Jewish religion. However, my exposure to Christianity was mostly negative. Every year just before Easter, I would go with my friends to the Church of the Holy Sepulcher, but not for spiritual enlightenment—we went to watch the priests fight one another. These fights usually turned violent, with priests pulling each other's hair or punching one another. Often, police would be called to intervene.

This was not my only picture of Christianity. The history of Jerusalem is filled with stories from the Crusades: European Christians killed Jews, Muslims, and Arab Christians alike, because of the assumption that anyone with dark skin was Muslim. In school I also learned about the "Christian" nations of Britain, Italy, and France, which violently colonized the Middle East. From American television I learned about western "Christian" culture and values. And so I came to understand that Christianity represented Westernization, dishonesty, immorality, lack of modesty, violence, and oppression.

I remember going to visit the Church of the Holy Sepulcher when I was sixteen years old. I walked into the church with a friend. We began to look around, trying to understand the meaning of the monument. Every year we saw thousands of tourists come to the church, and we saw many people crying and bending down to kiss stones in the building, but no one had ever told us why the church was important. On this day, a man who worked in the church approached us and asked if we were Christian. I told him no, and he asked us to leave the church. Later I came to understand that this was where Christians believed Jesus was crucified and rose from the dead. However, on that day all I learned was that Christianity was exclusive, and definitely not for me.

When Life Collides with Theology

Many people ask me how I became a Christian. I am glad to be able to share my story, but I must report that it was not a simple process, and telling the story does not make for a short answer! The best way to describe it is by saying that life collided with my theology. Here is how it happened.

As a child I never understood the Israeli-Palestinian conflict. For a kid it is complicated, hard to process. I knew we didn't like the Israelis. I knew I should run away whenever I saw an Israeli soldier, because they might shoot me. But I didn't understand the details. I wondered to myself, What is the difference between us and them?

I remember my mom waking me up at 2:00 one morning. She rushed us all up to the roof, where we hid in the darkness. A group of Israeli settlers were attacking our neighborhood in revenge because of a Palestinian who had stabbed an Israeli in Jerusalem. We hid on the roof for two hours, horrified, listening to the mob breaking windows, overturning cars, and destroying anything they could find. Yet in my young mind I did not worry. I found it exciting, as I wondered why there was a problem. But soon this childish innocence changed.

In the spring of 1990 we celebrated Ramadan, just like every other year, with fasting and family gatherings. I was nine years old. My parents woke my brothers and me up at 3:30 for an early breakfast, to fill us up before the sun rose and the fast started. At 4:00 we all went back to bed, stomachs full and happy.

The door burst open at 5:00 am, and Israeli soldiers stormed into our home. They pulled me and my brothers out of bed, and pointed their guns in our faces. They screamed at us, took our identity cards, and questioned all of us. "Where were you yesterday? Did you throw stones?" They demanded answers, and when they received none, they grabbed my brother Tayseer. My mother pleaded desperately with the soldiers, but in the end they took Tayseer with them. He was the brother closest to me in age, and at 18 years old was just finishing school.

For the first terrible days after that night, we did not know where they had taken him. Later, we found that he had been taken to an Israeli prison. He was held without trial, interrogated and tortured for fifteen days, until he admitted that he had thrown stones at Israeli cars. He was sent to a containment center indefinitely.

Over the next eleven months we were able to visit him three times. The closest we were able to get to him was through two fences, where countless other families lined up to shout across the yard at their sons. Even from a distance, though, it was clear that his health was deteriorating from repeated beatings. Finally, in the late days of March, he was released from prison in critical condition. His internal organs were badly damaged and he was throwing up blood. We rushed him to the hospital.

Tayseer held on for about three weeks, before dying after surgery. I was ten years old. Tayseer had been not only closest to me in age, but also closest to me as a friend and brother. I could not accept his death. He had been my mentor, helping me with homework and helping my mother raise me. He had been with me on my first day of school.

I became extremely bitter and angry at everything—at God, at people, and at life. Even at ten I understood that his death was not natural, and someone was responsible. I grew up with anger burning in my heart. I wanted justice. I wanted revenge. While my family decided to move on in life, I did not, and I was consumed with hatred.

When I got to high school I found a way to express my bitterness: I got involved in Palestinian politics. In politics I was able to carry out some petty revenge through writing. I became the editor of a political magazine designed for and directed at the youth groups of a political movement. My writings were full of animosity, and they expressed all the anger in my heart. I wanted to pass my anger on like a fire to as many people as possible. In many ways this became my life's passion, and I became a prisoner to these feelings.

After some time, I felt that the burden of my hate was too

heavy. I tried to run away from my pain by leaving the country. My grades were good enough to get scholarships to emigrate, but God did not allow it. I graduated from high school, and found myself stuck in Israel. I had refused to learn Hebrew growing up: it was the "enemy language." Now, to attend university or get a good job, I would have to compromise. I started studying in the Hebrew *Ulpan* (the institute for Jewish newcomers to Israel, where they learn proper Hebrew).

The Hebrew class was one of the hardest experiences I ever faced. It was the first time I had sat in a room of Jews who were not superior to me. It was the first time I had seen faces different from those of the soldiers at the checkpoints. Those soldiers had taken my brother; these students were the same as me. My understanding of the Jewish people started to collapse after just a few weeks at the Ulpan. I found myself confused, thinking, "How can they be normal human beings, just like me?" I was amazed that I could build friendships with these students and share their struggles. We went out for coffee together. We studied together. Sometimes we even found that we shared the same interests. For me, this was a turning point in my life. I came to understand that unfortunate things happen in our lives which are out of our control. A nine-year-old could not control the soldiers who took his brother. But now as an adult, I could control my response to these hurts. They had acted unjustly and murdered Tayseer, but I had the choice to follow in the same direction or to choose a new path.

A Different Kind of Christianity

It is amazing how God can use tragedies in our lives to lead us to Him. In my Hebrew class was a cute blonde American girl. We had a few conversations but were not good friends. However, one day while we were on break she told me that she knew how to sing in Arabic. I was interested. She started singing, but I did not understand a word she said. Her Arabic was bad, and I spoke limited English. She said something about her singing, and I thought she was inviting me to a concert. She said it was free, so I decided to go.

I remember arriving to the YMCA ready for a concert. The meeting began with singing in Arabic, with the words "I have decided to follow Jesus." I felt suddenly very uncomfortable. I didn't want to stay but was embarrassed to leave halfway through the service. As the meeting continued, a man stood up to preach. The message was translated to Hebrew and Arabic, and the sermon was one that I will never forget. This was the sermon that changed my life. It was entitled, "Love your neighbor."

The idea of loving your neighbor is not a popular message in Israel or Palestine. But as the minister preached about loving our neighbors and our enemies, I was amazed. This was a different kind of Christianity than I knew, and a different kind of religion than I was used to. The people were friendly, and they did not treat me differently because I was Arab. Moreover, there were both Arabs and Jews worshiping together in the church. This is an anomaly in Israel, where even Christian churches are often segregated. (Later I learned that many people in Israel and Palestine refuse to come to this particular congregation because it is mixed!)

A few days later I was given a Bible as a gift from one of the members of the church. He suggested that I start reading the book of John (now my favorite book in the Bible), and as I did, I had many questions about what I was reading. We started meeting every day to study the Bible. I was amazed at the lives of my new friends. One was an Arab-American Christian, and the other was a Jewish-British Christian. Both lived together in the same house! This was not normal in the world I lived in. The two men took time to teach me English, and as they did they taught me how to read the Bible. In the first month of studying with me, they did not challenge Islam or speak badly about my religion. They only answered my questions, prayed with me and taught me about Jesus. Their strategy was not to convince me of anything or to attack Islam. Their goal was to show me Christ, and they believed that with learning about Christ, I would understand the difference between Islam and Christianity.

A Change of Mind to Match a Change of Heart

I have often witnessed Christians reaching out to Muslims. Often it starts by Christians attacking or bad-mouthing Islam just minutes after the beginning of the conversation. I have never seen it work. Here are some of the things that affected me:

1. *Belief in the Bible*

Muslims believe in the Bible, but are convinced that it was changed. This belief comes from the Qur'an (see sura 2:75). I had the same belief. As a Muslim, I believed that Jesus was a great prophet, but the Christians changed the Bible to make it say what they wanted, by adding and subtracting passages from Scripture.

As I started studying the Bible, it raised many questions. I began spending more time seeking answers from the Qur'an, but I only became more confused. The Qur'an suggests that at the time of Muhammad (630 AD), truthful copies of the Bible still existed. Consider the following verse:

"It is He who sent down to thee (step by step), in truth, the Book, confirming what came before him; and He sent down the Law (of Moses) and the Gospel (of Jesus) before this, as a guide to mankind, and He sent down the criterion of judgment between right and wrong." (sura 3:3)

This verse suggests that the Qur'an came to confirm what already existed at the time of Muhammad. Take note that many English versions of the Qur'an translate the passage as "confirming what came before him." However the Arabic is clear and translates the phrase more accurately as "believing what is in his hands." My question was this: if Muhammad felt that the copy of the Bible "in his hands" was worthy of belief, then how could he argue that it had changed? We have many Biblical manuscripts which predate Islam by hundreds of years. These copies are the same as we read today, and were the same at the time of Muhammad. This logic made me question the Islamic view that the Bible had been changed.

While I was researching these verses, I remember asking the Jewish Christian why he decided to follow Christ. He directed me to Isaiah 53, an Old Testament scripture that prophesies Jesus' crucifixion. I asked him, "So this is the Jewish Bible?" He answered yes. Without thinking twice, I asked, "So why don't the Jews believe in Jesus? This is clearly talking about Christ." He was quick to answer me, "The question is why don't *you* believe?"

It challenged my faith. If the Jews changed their Bible as the Qur'an insists, wouldn't they take away prophecies about Jesus? I was convinced that at least the Old Testament was unchanged.

2. *The Cross*

The story of the cross is disputed in the Qur'an. Muslims believe that Jesus was taken to heaven before the crucifixion, and therefore did not die on the cross or resurrect from the dead. So what brought me to believe in the cross?

As I mentioned in my story, I grew up a good Muslim boy who prayed five times a day, fasted the month of Ramadan, attended the mosque on a regular basis, and memorized most of the Qur'an. I tried my best to be a good person. However, early in my childhood I understood that I could never be good enough. Islam as a religion is built on a credit system. According to Qur'an (sura 21:47 etc) also the Hadith:

> Narrated Abdullah ibn Amr: The Prophet (Peace Be Upon Him) said: There are two qualities or characteristics which will not be returned by any Muslim without his entering Paradise. While they are easy, those who act upon them are few. One should say: "Glory be to Allah" ten times after every prayer, "Praise be to Allah" ten

times and "Allah is Most Great" ten times. That is a hundred and fifty on the tongue, but one thousand and five hundred on the scale. When he goes to bed, he should say: "Allah is Most Great" thirty-four times, "Praise be to Allah" thirty-three times, and Glory be to Allah thirty-three times, for that is a hundred on the tongue and a thousand on the scale.

As a Muslim, I believed that God would have a scale, and would weigh our deeds. If the good deeds outweighed the bad, the person would be rewarded with heaven, and if the bad deeds outweighed the good, then the punishment would be hell.

In addition to this, I knew that repentance was not enough in Islam. I had to pay for sins or balance the scale by doing something good. I had to redeem myself from my sins. Consider the following Hadith, narrated by Abu Huraira:

A person had sexual relations with his wife in the month of Ramadan (while he was fasting), and he came to Allah's Apostle seeking his verdict concerning that action. The Prophet said (to him), "Can you afford to manumit a slave?" The man said, "No." The Prophet said, "Can you fast for two successive months?" He said, "No." The Prophet said, "Then feed sixty poor persons." (Sahih Bukhari)

In Christianity, you cannot make up for your sin. You are only required to repent, or to change your heart and mind. There is no deed that you can do to make it even. It is only through Christ's sacrifice that you are cleansed. This knowledge gave me a kind of relief and peace that I had never felt before: all my life, I had been trying to redeem myself when it was impossible. At last, a solution that made sense.

"For all have sinned and fall short of the glory of God, and are justified freely by his grace through the redemption that came by Christ Jesus" (Romans 3:23–24).

3. Forgiveness

As I started understanding the cross and how central it is in Christian life, I realized that I had to deal with my heart and confront my prejudice, hatred, and bitterness. I started to learn about forgiveness, which had seemed impossible to me all my life. I realized that believing in Jesus meant living like him. This included forgiving those who sinned against me. I knew that I needed forgiveness for my own sins, but I still did not want to forgive the soldiers that killed my brother.

After being in the church for a while, my heart began to change. I was becoming friends with Christians who were both Arabs and Jews. I was making new friends in my Hebrew class. In response to these changes, I decided I would not hate all the Jews or all the soldiers, but reserve my hatred for those who killed my brother. I wouldn't give that up. I felt that to give up hatred for my brother's killers would be tantamount to betraying or abandoning my brother.

"And when you stand praying, if you hold anything against anyone, forgive him, so that your Father in heaven may forgive you your sins. But if you do not forgive, neither will your Father who is in heaven forgive your sins" (Mark 11:25).

I had so many sins for which I needed forgiveness. Still, I didn't believe that I could forgive others. I had good reasons to hate and I couldn't just overlook them. But it was tearing my heart apart. How could I betray my heart? How could I betray the blood of my brother? I felt it was impossible, that I would never forgive. Yet what is impossible for man is possible with God.

What Helped Me to Forgive?

First of all, Jesus expects his followers to forgive others as he forgives them. There are no exceptions. If I wanted to be forgiven, I needed to forgive. That was hard to accept. I prayed that God would open my eyes so that I could see who I really was. For some time, instead of moving towards forgiveness, I moved toward ignorance and deceit. I thought I had forgiven, but I only deceived myself and justified my sin. I told myself it was normal to be a little bitter and that I don't have to forgive completely. Jesus, however, gave me full forgiveness and I couldn't do any less. When I learned that my sin killed Jesus, I knew that I was guilty of murder as well. I killed someone innocent who loved me and wanted the best for me. With my sins, I am in no way better than those who killed my brother. I am a sinner and need forgiveness as much as they do.

Second, Jesus understood that forgiveness is not easy. It does not come naturally. Jesus had to go to the cross to achieve forgiveness for me. I have to go to the cross as well to forgive others. During the last days of Jesus' life on earth, he offered up prayers and petitions with loud cries and tears to the one who could save him from death, and he was heard because of his reverent submission. I knew from Islam that submission was important, and I saw that Jesus learned obedience from what he suffered (Hebrews 5:7–8).

In Luke 22:41–44, Jesus had to suffer to achieve forgiveness, so we have to expect and accept that forgiveness will also be painful for us. Despite the pain of being betrayed, spat on, and treated without mercy, Jesus did not give in to Satan, but sought help from the Father. Although he was distressed when he went to the cross, he did not let this keep him from submitting to God. As I carried my cross of forgiveness I had to remember Jesus. He prayed with tears. He told God that it was hard for him to carry the cross, but he still went through with it.

(Often in the church we face the same thing: We get hurt and bitter and angry, but we have to make a choice to forgive exactly as Jesus did. Forgiveness is not between us and the church; it is between us and God. We are responsible before God to forgive others completely and unconditionally. He forgave us fully, but this was only possible because he denied himself and went to the cross to accomplish it. We need to make the same decision in our lives: We need to go to the cross so we can forgive those who have hurt us.)

Now, ten years later, I realize that the decision to forgive is not a one-day event. The decision to forgive is something I have to struggle with on daily basis. Every time I cross a checkpoint, every time I think about being forced to leave my home, every time I struggle with having to leave my country to come to the United States, and every time I see the news from Israel, I have to forgive. My brother's picture is on the mantel in our home, and every time I look at that picture I have to forgive. Each day I live I refuse to become like those soldiers fifteen years ago, and each day I must renew my choice to put aside the resentment and rage I nursed as a teenager. I will always have this choice. It is a hard decision to abandon revenge, and an easy road to follow your feelings. Yet hatred begets hatred, and as we do to others, so will it be done to us. As a result, each day I must choose again to love and forgive those around me.

When I finally chose to forgive fully, my actions followed my heart. I became a peacemaker. For a number of years I worked with an organization of Israelis and Palestinians who decided to put anger aside and work for peace, despite great personal losses. I decided to counter the hatred by meeting people face to face. Since then, my work has been to educate people on the human and moral costs of the conflict. In this line of work, I have visited hundreds of Israeli and Palestinian classrooms, countless churches, mosques, and synagogues, and scores of universities around the world, including Yale, Georgetown, Princeton, and others. At these lectures I work to tear down the wall of stereotypes that people put between themselves and the "other side."

Almost every time I speak in the Israeli community, the majority of people I meet have never met a Palestinian. When I speak in the Palestinian community, the story is the same: most Palestinians have never met an Israeli, apart from Israeli soldiers. These lectures are never easy. The audience is often angry, and has many accusations, assumptions, and arguments about why they cannot cooperate with the other side.

Despite their anger and bitterness, most Israelis and Palestinians want the conflict to end and to live in peace. The problem is that being a peace activist is hard work, and attracts a lot of persecution. I have suffered humiliation at checkpoints, waiting for hours at a time and strip-searched on my way to lecture on peace. I have been spat upon and beaten just for my ethnicity. However, these hardships are small when compared to all the blessings God has given me as part of his promise, "Blessed are the peacemakers."

Jesus Is Lord

Even after all these changes, one of the hardest things for a Muslim to accept is that Jesus is Lord. One of the first verses in Qur'an I memorized was:

"Say: He is Allah, the One and Only; Allah, the Eternal, Absolute; He begets not, nor is He begotten; and there is none like unto Him."

This passage is engraved in the mind of every Muslim. God cannot have a son. God is higher than having a son. How can the Most High have a son? It is unimaginable for God Almighty to have a son.

Studying the Bible, I faced a tough decision. My heart was changing, but I still didn't want to change the way I thought about God. I realized that I had limited God to what is appropriate in man's logic. As a Muslim, I had understood that God cannot have a son because I didn't think it was appropriate for him to do so. My God was limited by man's wisdom, and God has no limits.

"For to us a child is born, to us a son is given, and the government will be on his shoulders. And he will be

called Wonderful Counselor, Mighty God, Everlasting
Father, Prince of Peace. Of the increase of his government and peace there will be no end. He will reign on
David's throne and over his kingdom, establishing and
upholding it with justice and righteousness from that
time on and forever. The zeal of the LORD Almighty will
accomplish this" (Isaiah 9:6–7).

Isaiah 9 was the scripture that brought me to full faith. It was
prophesied seven hundred years before Christ was even born
that God would be incarnated on earth. He would be God with
us. He would be our counselor, our father, our Prince of Peace,
and the king who will rule forever!

Converted

After intensive Bible study lasting for four months, I was
convinced. Jesus was (and is!) Lord, and I had to become a
Christian. However, there was one more problem.

"Abdullah (b. Mas'ud) reported: Allah's Messenger (may
peace be upon him) stood up and said: By Him besides
Whom there is no god but He, the blood of a Muslim
who bears the testimony that there is no god but Allah,
and I am His Messenger, may be lawfully shed only in
case of three persons: the one who abandons Islam,
and deserts the community [Ahmad, one of the narra-
tors, is doubtful whether the Holy Prophet (may peace
be upon him) used the word li'l-jama'ah or al-jama'ah],
and the married adulterer, and life for life" (*Book 016,
Hadith 4154, Sahih Muslim*).

I have studied the Bible with many Muslims who came to
faith in Christ but would not go all the way because of fear. They
protest that they can lose friends, family, job, house, money,
and even life. Is it worth it? Unfortunately, many Muslims
decide not to endanger themselves by becoming Christians.

But for me, becoming a Christian was the wisest thing I ever did.

I suffered for it. I was beaten and thrown out of the house when my family even suspected I was studying the Bible. Ultimately, they simply denied my change and worked hard to keep it from reaching the community at large. When I invited people to church in the streets, they told the neighbors it was for my job. When I tried to convince them of Christianity, they ignored me and said I was an atheist. (In the Islamic community, it is better to be an atheist than a convert!)

My conversion has shaped the rest of my life. No longer do I live in guilt, but by faith. I am not living my life focused on my deeds, hoping that I can be good enough to make it to heaven. I now know that only through grace and love I am redeemed. I am finally able to counter hatred with love because I understand that God loved me even when I was disobedient and a sinner. I feel free from the chains of this world, the chains of sin and the chains of hypocrisy. I am now able to be myself before God and men.

I still have a dream for my family and for my people. I pray for them, and desire that God will lead them to the same path he showed me. My sister has read the Bible and we have been talking about it. Two of my brothers have attended church. Becoming Christian didn't make Muslims my enemies. If anything, I now have more compassion and more love for the Muslim people, because they are my lost family, my friends and my people, and it is my mission to bring the gospel to them.

A Final Word

In my travels, I have met many Christians who have repeated scholarly sounding ideas about Islam, and scholarly sounding ideas about the Middle East. However, in reality, few of these people had any basis for their opinions aside from American media and books. These same people always seem to believe it is too hard to reach out to Muslims. I am thankful that in *Jesus and Islam,* Douglas Jacoby has taken the time

to learn the truth about this major world faith. He has studied the Qur'an, interacted with Muslims, and pushed himself
to objectively grasp the facts about Islam. He goes out of his
way not to misrepresent Muslims, and is quick to receive input
from insiders.

I have seen Douglas' faith in action. Over a decade ago I
met Douglas when I was a young Muslim studying the Bible.
At that time I was able to ask him questions about Christianity, and his compassionate and patient responses helped me in
my journey to become a Christian. Since then, Douglas and I
have become good friends, and he has visited Jerusalem many
times. I have often watched him interact with the Muslim community in Jerusalem, and he has always impressed me with
his wisdom in "speaking the truth in love." Even with my very
opinionated, argumentative father, Douglas was able to have
a great conversation about Christianity and earn his respect.

Every time I enter the bookstore I find myself in the religion section. I always check what is new on Islam, and I am
always disappointed by writers who spend much of their book
attacking Islam on criteria that they would never use when
judging the Bible. I believe we ought to be honest with ourselves and with the people around us, and although we don't
believe that Islam is a message from God, we must judge it by
the same standards that we use to evaluate the Bible: respect
for historical context, linguistic study, and narrative analysis.
Moreover, we should judge a religion first by its own tenets,
and only then by its adherents. Many of them are genuine in
their faith, and seeking God in the best way they know.

Still, beginning to understand Islam comes not from
accumulating knowledge, but through love, compassion and
care. This is how God reached out to us: not by the wisdom of
the world, but by the unconditional love—death on the cross
for his enemies. As one old adage goes, people don't care how
much you know until they know how much you care. This is
why I came to church, and this is why I decided to study the
Bible. I would never have gone back to a church where I didn't

feel care and love. I was blessed to have people who believed that Muslims can become Christians, and I was blessed by God to meet people who rejected prejudice and embraced me with the grace of God, teaching me the Word.

My deepest thanks go out to those men and women who had a heart for reaching Muslims—they are the peacemakers and heroes of this world.

Appendix:

Appendix:
The Structure of the Qur'an

No.	Arabic name	English name	Verses
1	Al-Fatihah	The opening	7
2	Al-Baqarah	The cow	286
3	Al-'Imran	The family of Imran	199
4	An-Nisa'	The women	177
5	Al-Ma'idah	The food	120
6	Al-An'am	The cattle	166
7	Al-A'raf	The elevated places	206
8	Al-Anfal	Voluntary gifts	75
9	At-Taubah	Repentance	129
10	Yunus	Jonah	109
11	Hud	A warning	123
12	Yusuf	Joseph	111
13	Ar-Ra'd	The thunder	43
14	Ibrahim	Abraham	52
15	Al-Hijr	The rock	99
16	An-Nahl	The bee	128
17	Al-Isra	The Israelites	111
18	Al-Kahf	The cave	110
19	Maryam	Mary	98
20	Tâ-Hâ	Ta-Ha	135
21	Al-Anbiyâ'	The prophets	112
22	Al-Hajj	The pilgrimage	78
23	Al-Mu'minûn	The criterion	118
24	An-Nûr	The light	64
25	Al-Furqân	The standard	77
26	Ash-Shu'arâ'	The poets	227

No.	Arabic name	English name	Verses
27	An-Naml	The ant	93
28	Al-Qasas	The stories	88
29	Al-'Ankabût	The spider	69
30	Ar-Rum	The Romans	60
31	Luqmân	Luqman	34
32	As-Sajdah	The adoration	30
33	Al-Ahzab	The allies	73
34	Saba'	Sheba	54
35	Fâtir	The originator	45
36	Yâ-Sîn	Ya-seen	83
37	As-Saffat	The ranks	182
38	Sad	(The letter) sad	88
39	Az-Zumar	The troops	75
40	Ghafir	The forgiver	85
41	Fussilat	Made plain	54
42	Ash-Shura	The counsel	53
43	Az-Zukhruf	Gold	89
44	Ad-Dukhan	The drought	59
45	Al-Jâthiya	The kneeling	37
46	Al-Ahqaf	The sand dunes	35
47	Muhammad	Muhammad	38
48	Al-Fath	The victory	29
49	Al-Hujurat	The apartments	18
50	Qaf	(The letter) qaf	50
51	Az-Zariyat	The scatterers	60
52	At-Tur	The mountain	49
53	An-Najm	The star	61
54	Al-Qamar	The moon	55
55	Ar-Rahman	The Beneficent	78
56	Al-Waqi''ah	The event	96
57	Al-Hadid	Iron	29
58	Al-Mujadilah	The pleading woman	22
59	Al-Hashr	Banishment	24
60	Al-Mumtahinah	She who is examined	13
61	As-Saff	Battle array	14
62	Al-Jumu'ah	The congregation	11
63	Al-Munafiqûn	The hypocrites	11
64	At-Taghâbun	Haggling	18
65	At-Talâq	Divorce	12
66	At-Tahrîm	The prohibition	12
67	Al-Mulk	The kingdom	30
68	Al-Qalam	The pen	52
69	Al-Hâqqah	The reality	52
70	Al-Ma'ârij	The ways of ascent	44

No.	Arabic name	English name	Verses
71	Nûh	Noah	28
72	Al-Jinn	The jinn (demons)	28
73	Al-Muzzammil	The enshrouded one	20
74	Al-Muddaththir	The cloaked one	56
75	Al-Qiyâmah	The resurrection	40
76	Al-Insân	The man	31
77	Al-Mursalât	The emissaries	50
78	An-Naba'	The announcement	40
79	An-Nâzi'ât	Those who yearn	46
80	'Abasa	He frowned	42
81	At-Takwîr	The folding up	29
82	Al-Infitâr	The cleaving	19
83	Al-Mutaffifin	The cheaters	36
84	Al-Inshiqâq	The splitting open	25
85	Al-Burûj	The constellations	22
86	At-Tarîq	The morning star	86
87	Al-A'lâ	The most high	19
88	Al-Ghâshiyah	The overwhelming	26
89	Al-Fajr	The daybreak	30
90	Al-Balad	The city	20
91	Ash-Shams	The sun	15
92	Al-Lail	The night	21
93	Adh-Dhuhâ	The morning hours	11
94	Ash-Sharh	Relief	8
95	At-Tîn	The fig	8
96	Al-'Alaq	The clot	19
97	Al-Qadr	The majesty	5
98	Al-Baiyinah	The clear evidence	8
99	Az-Zalzalah	The earthquake	8
100	Al-'Adiyât	The chargers	11
101	Al-Qâri'ah	The calamity	11
102	At-Takâthur	Abundance	8
103	Al-'Asr	The time	3
104	Al-Humazah	The slanderer	9
105	Al-Fîl	The elephant	5
106	Al-Quraysh	The shark	4
107	Al-Mâ'ûn	Acts of kindness	7
108	Al-Kauthar	Plenty	3
109	Al-Kâfirûn	The disbelievers	6
110	An-Nasr	The help	3
111	Al-Masad	The flame	5
112	Al-Ikhlâs	The unity	112
113	Al-Falaq	The dawn	5
114	An-Nas	Mankind	6

Notes

Chapter One—The Challenge

[1] Or, as someone else astutely put it, "He who throws dirt loses ground."

[2] In the Qur'an, the *sura* is the chapter, while the *aya* (plural *ayat*) is the verse or sentence.

[3] L. Saad, "Anti-Muslim Sentiments Fairly Commonplace" (Gallup Poll News Service), 10 August 2006.

[4] C.S. Lewis, *God in the Dock* (Grand Rapids: Eerdmans, 1960). This book includes 48 essays and 12 letters written between 1940 and 1963 for a wide variety of publications.

[5] In academia, the common view of sociology and anthropology is that since all religious beliefs are culturally conditioned, none are true. Faith is merely a product of upbringing and social conditioning. But this so-called logic hardly proves that these faiths are all false. Here is why: The person affirming that *others'* beliefs are culturally conditioned is *also* the product of a certain conditioning. Yet that person would not let us conclude that *his* or *her* observations, therefore, are spurious. In other words, the insights of anthropology and the sociology of religion must be carefully weighed, for they are occasionally misguided and even self-refuting.

[6] To drive the point home, when addressing an audience, I will sometimes ask, "Is anyone named John here? Would you please stand up?" Depending on the size of the audience, we will have two, ten or even twenty Johns standing. Speaking facetiously, I explain to the audience that, really, all these Johns are the same person. "They're all masculine hominid bipeds," I jest, "with skin, ears, and a nose." But these similarities are superficial; we easily distinguish one John from another. In the same way, common terminology does not necessarily

prove common identity of meaning. One "god" is not necessarily the same god as another.

[7] One of the more unusual reference books is *Encyclopedia of Gods: Over 2,500 Deities of the World*, by Michael Jordan (New York: Facts on File, 1993).

[8] Interestingly, most who claim to be tolerant are quite intolerant of any who disagree with them, as many apologists, logicians and philosophers have pointed out. For example, see Paul Copam, *True for You but Not for Me* (Bloomington, Minn: Bethany, 1998).

[9] As a theology student at Harvard, I was able to study under some of the world's top scholars at the prestigious Center for the Study of World Religions. My first course: a year of Indian, Tibetan, Chinese and Japanese Buddhism. Despite occasional parallels, how different the flavors and stripes of Buddhism are compared to Christianity and Judaism! And Islam is poles apart from Hinduism, Wicca, and the New Age Movement!

Chapter Two—Overview

[10] Several gods worshiped in Arabia during Muhammad's time are named in sura 71:23. These are *Wadd, Suwa', Yaghuth, Ya'uq*, and *Nasr.*

[11] For example: Sura 57:27 denounces monasticism, a common feature of Christianity.

[12] Zoroastrianism, a religion founded in the sixth century BC, was the state religion of Persia. Arabia at this time was neither part of the Roman Empire nor the Persian Empire. The Zoroastrians are referred to in sura 22:17.

[13] Manichees were followers of Mani, a third-century AD Syrian prophet who proclaimed a radical dualism—the powers of darkness striving to overthrow the powers of light. His teachings spread eastward through Persia, all the way to China.

[14] This was somewhat like the move of Jacob's family to Egypt in Exodus 1:1-5.

[15] To convert the hijrah year to AD, divide by 1.031 and add 622. To go the other way, from AD to hijrah, subtract 622, then multiply by 1.031. The odd multiplier is because the Muslim year is 354 days, based on a lunar calendar with exactly 12 cycles. The shortfall means 11 days are lost each year, or 1 year every 32 Hijri years. Each new month begins not with the new moon, but with a crescent moon. The *crescent* moon, derived from the old polytheism (moon worship), is a common Muslim symbol.

[16] The hijrah is similar to Abraham's move from Haran to the

Promised Land, some two-and-a-half millennia earlier, as a departure from a place of entrenched idolatry. It also resembles the Exodus of the Hebrews from Egypt, which took place about two millennia before the Hijrah.

[17] The experts admit defeat; no one knows the origins of this word.

[18] http://www.qur'an.org/ap28.htm contradicts this view, based on 29:48. Moreover, in 25:5 we read, "They also said, 'Tales from the past that he wrote down; they were dictated to him day and night.'" For this reason some Muslims say Muhammad was illiterate before 610 AD, and then received (miraculously) the gift of literacy. Yet it may be asked, would a merchant be completely illiterate? We would expect at least a rudimentary ability to write down names, products, and numbers.

[19] Such as Asma bin Marwan and Abu 'Afak, two of his opponents in Medina.

[20] For more names, see http://www.dawateislami.net/GENERAL/devotions/99NAMES/M-index.htm.

[21] Henceforth only the sura and verse number will be given, thus indicating that the source is the Qur'an.

[22] This is supported by 21:27: "They precede Him not in speech, and only according to His commandment do they act." While this aya appears to describe the *general* obedience and faithfulness of the prophets, some Muslims interpret it in the strictest possible way. They claim sinlessness for all God's messengers. And if for all, how much more for Muhammad, the greatest of Allah's messengers!

[23] To further explore Buddhism, see www.buddhanet.net.

[24] As to being a divine sage, or even a good man, far be it from me to make any such claim!" (Analects 7:33).

[25] Interestingly, although many Christian churches advocate the Jewish custom of tithing, or giving away 10% of one's income, most church members give just over 2% of their gross earnings to the church. Data Source: *The State of Church Giving through 2003* (15th ed.), Empty Tomb, Inc. 2005.

[26] The Shi'ites believe in 20% because of a Quranic verse (8:41) on the spoils of war. They extend the principle to seven further areas: buried or hidden treasure; mines and minerals; sea treasures obtained by diving, such as pearls; halal money mixed with non-halal money; land bought by a non-Muslim; and surplus annual profits.

[27] Bukhari (died 870 AD) was one of several who compiled the Hadith. He examined some 300,000 hadith, of which he deemed 200,000 to be unsupported. Of the remaining 100,000, he accepted some 10,000 as authoritative. Even with only 10,000 hadith, the

effective scriptural base of Islam had vastly increased.

Moreover, this is the way all religions operate. Their authoritative texts are read through the filter of the group's traditions. Thus, the Jews have their Torah but also the Mishnah; the Christians have their Bible but also their creeds and traditions. The hadith supporting five daily prayers is found in Bukhari, *Book of the Times of Prayer*, Ch.5.

[28] A mosque is generally carpeted, free of furniture (which could impede the motion of prostration), and free of images. Many mosques effectively serve as community places, and are used as educational centers, venues for political discussion, etc. Women are always separated from the men—for example, behind a screen, standing behind them, meeting at different times of the day, etc.

[29] McDermott, Gerald R. *Can Evangelicals Learn from World Religions?* (Downers Grove, Illinois: Intervarsity, 2000),

[30] From 622, the official start year for Islam, Muslims prayed facing Jerusalem. In 624 the city was changed to Mecca.

[31] There is no evidence for this claim. In fact, the meteorite was actually a center of ancient idolatry before the arrival of the Muslim religion, as Muslim scholars freely admit. When Islam was finally accepted in Mecca, the traditional place of worship was kept, possibly as an integrating point, to ease the people's transition to the new religion.

[32] The Sunni branch believes that the first four caliphs— Muhammad's successors—rightfully took his place as leaders of Muslims, and the heirs of these caliphs are the legitimate leaders, ruling in unbroken succession in the Arab world until the breakup of the Ottoman Empire following World War I. In contrast, Shi'ites believe that only the heirs of the fourth caliph, Ali, are Muhammad's legitimate successors. In addition, there are other differences. Sunnis emphasize Allah's sovereignty in the discussion of predestination in the Qur'an, while the Shi'ite understanding emphasizes the role of individual free will. (This mirrors the Calvinist versus Arminian debate in Christianity.)

[33] For the sake of comparison, According to David Barrett et al, editors of the World Christian Encyclopedia: A comparative survey of churches and religions—AD 30 to 2200, "There are 19 major world religions which are subdivided into a total of 270 large religious groups, and many smaller ones. 34,000 separate Christian groups have been identified in the world." Over half of them are independent churches that are not interested in linking with the big denominations.

[34] See http://godlas.myweb.uga.edu/sufismintro.html.

[35] The technical term for tongues is *glossolalia.* I have heard many

"tongue-speakers" many times, but have never been convinced that it is actually a miracle. In my religious past, I even learned how to fake "tongues." Linguists are agreed that glossolalia is not actual language. For more on this, please see my book *The Spirit* (Spring, TX: Illumination Publishers International, 2005).

[36] The Muslims would eventually become very powerful in India during later Mughal times (1556-1857). Interestingly, the Hindus were treated as "people of the book," not because ordinary Hindus were monotheists (they are not!), but because many Hindu philosophers, who came into contact with Muslim thinkers, were.

[37] On one of my visits to the Philippines, I was privileged to speak in Mindanao. Many Westerners avoid this sometimes troubled region, yet the people of Mindanao are warm, kind, and, for the most part, peace-loving. I say for the most part because it only takes a small minority to sully the reputation of the large majority.

[38] This verse is almost exactly the same as 5:69. See also 22:40.

[39] Many commentators say this refers only to those Jews and Christians who convert to Islam.

[40] I recently led a biblical study group to western Turkey. Although Haghia Sophia, built in the 500s, was built considerably later than the period in which we were interested, we visited this amazing structure. It was once a church, then a mosque, then a church again—a common pattern in lands where religion seesawed according to the vicissitudes of politics. Ironically, Istanbul is where the Greek Orthodox church is headquartered, even though Turkey is 99% Muslim. It is a vestige of the old Byzantine Empire (c. 330-1453).

[41] Source: 2001 census (2.7%).

[42] 0.6% of the population of the United States are Muslims, according to the CIA *World Factbook.*

[43] The Nation of Islam (NOI) was founded in 1930 by Wallace Fard. The three fundamental principles of NOI are: Allah is God; the white man is the devil; the black man is the cream of the planet earth.

In 1934 Elijah Muhammad took the reins of the NOI, challenging Fard's divine inspiration. The NOI was renamed and reorganized as a Sunni organization by Warith Deen Muhammad in 1975, but Louis Farrakhan has reestablished the organization along the original Fardian lines.

[44] If you are interested in learning about their teachings firsthand, you can, of course, visit the headquarters of the Nation of Islam in Chicago. You could also phone them, or visit their website, www.finalcall.com. But as you do your research, be sure to get the other side's perspective. I would recommend an article by A. I. Palmer,

"The Nation of Islam Exposed," found online at www.geocities.com/athens/olympus/4222/noi.html.

[45] The science of stratigraphy, embryonic in Ibn Sina's observations, would be fully developed by eighteenth-century Europeans.

[46] In the New World, the value of having a place-holder to represent zero was also discovered by the Mayans.

[47] This is not, however, to say that science under the Muslims flourished in a coherent or systematic way. The birth of modern science took place in Europe, not Africa or the Middle East.

[48] Except for sura 9. According to Uthman, the ninth chapter was essentially part of the eighth.

[49] Or "Beneficent."

[50] For example, 4:100 and 110:3.

[51] Moreover, the words of the eighth-century Sufi poem by Rabi'a al-Adawiya come near to a Christian understanding of grace. "O my Lord, if I worship Thee from fear of Hell, burn me in Hell, and if I worship Thee in hope of Paradise, exclude me thence, but if I worship Thee for Thine own sake, then withhold not from me Thine Eternal Beauty."

[52] And yet Hadith B 97:24 claims that Allah exercises his mercy towards those who have done nothing to deserve it.

[53] One is reminded of Judges 6:31, where Joash throws down the challenge to Ba'al to defend himself—if he really is a god. Or of Rabbi Gamaliel's wise counsel in Acts 5:38-39.

[54] John L. Esposito and Dalia Mogahed, *Who Speaks for Islam?* (New York: Gallup Press, 2007), 38-39.

[55] Not to say that the draconian sentence is always carried out. On 20 October 2008, the government of Afghanistan commuted the death sentence of a "blasphemer" to 20 years' incarceration. Some sects of Islam, like the Ismailis, reject this practice altogether. Capital punishment for apostasy applies to (sane) adult males. There are of course occasional exceptions. In 2007 the Grand Mufti of Egypt allowed Muslims to change their faith, proclaiming that such will be accountable to Allah at the Day of Judgment, and so should not be punished in this life.

[56] "Ex-Moslems Explain 'Why I Chose Jesus,'" from the editors of *Religion Today*, "Current News Source" (April 11, 2001). Cited at www.crosswalk.com/525428.

[57] The Red Crescent Society now works in cooperation with the Red Cross. Combined, there are currently some 97 million volunteers worldwide.

[58] Galatians 5:22-23.

[59] Matthew 5:13-14.

[60] C.S. Lewis (1898-1963), Oxford and Cambridge scholar, expert in English Literature, converted from atheism and became a champion of the Christian faith.

[61] From Phillip Yancey's excellent book, *What's So Amazing about Grace?* (Grand Rapids: Zondervan, 1997). Yancey credits Calvin College professor Scott Hoezee for this story (*The Riddle of Grace: Applying God's Grace to the Christian Life*. Grand Rapids: Eerdmans, 1996). Hoezee told me he heard it from Peter Kreeft, professor of philosophy at Boston College and The King's College. When I contacted Kreeft, he said that he had "heard or read" this account but did not remember where. He added, "My version said 'the forgiveness of sins' rather 'than 'grace,' but that would not be quite correct since Judaism has this too." Sleuth-work has its limits. Apocryphal or genuine? For students of Lewis, the story certainly rings true.

Chapter Three—Al-Qur'an

[62] This reminds us of ancient times, when Christians in Greco-Roman society were commonly called atheists. An atheist was someone who denied the gods, and since Christians did not believe in the gods, they were called atheists. And yet, in a way, nothing could have been further from the truth!

[63] Muhammad ibn Ishaq, Muhammad's first biographer, writes about Muhammad's strange encounter on the Hira' mountain:

"I was lying asleep, when an angel came to me with a piece of material and said, 'Read this [recite].'
I replied, 'I cannot read.'
Then he pressed the material against me so hard that I thought I would die. Then he let me go and said again, 'Read.'
The angel repeated his command once more.
Nervously I replied, 'What am I to read?'
The angel said, 'Read in the name of your Lord. He who created and made man from an embryo [clot of blood]. Read, for your Lord is merciful like no one on earth. He who instructed men by the pen—He taught him what he did not know.'
I awoke from my sleep, and it was as if these words were written in my heart. I came out of the cave and stood on the mountainside. Then I heard a voice calling to me from heaven: 'Muhammad, you are God's messenger and I am Gabriel...'"

[64] See sura 13:27; 20:113; 26:195; 39:28; 41:3,44; 42:7; 43:1; 46:12.

[65] See sura 43:3-4: "Surely We have made it an Arabic Qur'an that you may understand. And it is in the Original of the book with Us, truly elevated, full of wisdom."

[66] Muslims believe that no sooner was Muhammad born than he reached down for some earth, flung it into the air, and proclaimed, "Great is Allah!" The various miracles attributed to Muhammad appear in the early 8th century, some 75-100 years after this death

[67] Ubay was not the only one who included these missing suras in his codex. Al-Suyuti related that Ibn Abbass and Abu Musa also included them as part of their texts (Al-Itqan, 154).

[68] For one website indicating how translations vary, see http://www.qurantoday.com/BaqSec37.htm. Following are some of the available versions: Muhammad Marmaduke William Pickthall, *The Meaning of the Glorious Qur'an* (1930); Abdullah Yusuf Ali, *The Holy Qur'an: Translation and Commentary* (1934 and 1937); Sher Ali, *The Holy Qur'an: Arabic Text with English Translation* (1955); Muhammad Asad, *The Message of the Qur'an: Translated and Explained* (1980); Sheikh Muhammad Sarwar, *The Holy Qur'an* (1981); Mohammad Habib Shakir, *The Holy Qur'an* (1983); Thomas Ballantyne Irving, *The Qur'an: First American Version*—Later editions titled *Holy Qur'an: the Noble Reading* (1985); Rashad Khalifa, *The Final Testament Authorized English Version Translated from the Original* (1992); Maulana Muhammad Ali, *The Holy Qur'an: Arabic Text, English Translation and Commentary* (1995); Amatul Rahman Omar and Abdul Mannan Omar, *The Holy Qur'an: Arabic Text—English Translation as explained by Allamah Nooruddin* (1997); Muhammad Farooq-i-Azam Malik, *Al-Qur'an, the Guidance for Mankind English with Arabic Text* (1997); Muhammad Taqi-ud-Din Al-Hilali and Muhammad Muhsin Khan, *Interpretation of the Meanings of The Noble Qur'an in the English Language: A Summarized Version of At-Tabari, Al-Qurtubi and Ibn Kathir with Comments from Sahih Al-Bukhari* (1998).

[69] *Twenty Three Years: A Study of the Prophetic Career of Mohammed*, translated from Persian by F. R. C. Bagley (London: George Allen & Unwin, 1985). The original manuscript was authored in 1937.

[70] From the Hadith of Bukhari (Hudud 24, 37). Although the Qur'an specifies 100 lashings for adultery, the Hadith require the adulterer to be stoned (Hadith of Bukhari 8806).

[71] Although this account was not in the original copies of John's gospel, it rings true and is generally accepted as authentic.

[72] The Gallup pollsters put many Muslims' feelings into words: "When we asked respondents in 10 predominantly Muslim countries how they view a number of nations, the attributes they most

associated with the United States are: ruthless (68%), scientifically and technologically advanced (68%), aggressive (66%), conceited (65%), and morally decadent (64%)." Further: "When Gallup asked the open-ended question, 'In your own words, what do you resent most about the West?' the most frequent response across all countries among moderates and radicals is 'sexual and cultural promiscuity,' followed by 'ethical and moral corruption' and 'hatred of Muslims.'" Source: John L. Esposito and Dalia Mogahed, *Who Speaks for Islam?* (New York: Gallup Press, 2007), 84, 88.

[73] In sura 53:32 we read, "They avoid gross sins and transgressions, except for minor offenses. Your Lord's forgiveness is immense. He has been fully aware of you since He initiated you from the earth, and while you were embryos in your mothers' bellies. Therefore, do not exalt yourselves; He is fully aware of the righteous." Also, sura 42:37 mentions "those who shun the great sins and indecencies..."

[74] These include 4:48,116; 5:722; 6:102,164; 7:173,191,195; 10:28,66,68; 12:38,106; 13:16,33,36; 14:30; 15:96; 16:51,54,57,86; 17:22,39-40,111; 18:4,15,42; 19:35,88-93; 21:26; 22:26,31; 23:55,91; 24:55; 25:2; 27:63; 29:8; 30:13; 34:22,27; 35:40; 39:67; 50:26; 51:51; 72:3; 112:1-4.

[75] Compare to the following versions:

(1) "The men are made responsible for the women, since GOD endowed them with certain qualities, and made them the bread earners. The righteous women will cheerfully accept this arrangement, and observe GOD's commandments, even when alone in their privacy. If you experience opposition from the women, you shall first talk to them, then (*you may use such negative incentives as*) deserting them in bed, then you may (*as a last alternative*) beat them (*in self-defense*). If they obey you, you are not permitted to transgress against them. GOD is Most High, Supreme." —*Qur'an: The Final Testament (Authorized English Version)*, tr. Rashad Khalifa (Tucson: Islamic Productions, 1989).

(2) "Men are the protectors and maintainers of women, because Allah has given the one more (strength) than the other, and because they support them from their means. Therefore the righteous women are devoutly obedient, and guard in (the husband's) absence what Allah would have them guard. As to those women on whose part ye fear disloyalty and ill-conduct, admonish them (first), (Next), refuse to share their beds, (And last) beat them (lightly); but if they return to obedience, seek not against them Means (of annoyance): For Allah is Most High, great (above you all)." —*The Holy Qur'an*, at http://www.islamicity.com/mosque/QUR'AN/4.htm.

[76] The context of this passage is important. To be fair, the text refers to women widowed and children orphaned in the war of Uhud. It reads, "And if you fear that you cannot do justice to orphans, marry such women as seem good to you, two, or three, or four; but if you fear that you will not do justice, then (marry) only one or that which your right hands possess. This is more proper that you may not do injustice."

[77] For more on the practice of sigeh, see: https://www.pbs.org/wgbh/pages/frontline/ tehranbureau/2010/03/temporary-marriage-and-the-economy-of-pleasure.html. For a women's perspective on Islam, see https://www.amazon.com/God-Who-Hates-Courageous-Inflamed/ dp/0312538367./

[78] See also Qur'an 78:32ff.

[79] Muslims claim, based on the Hadith, that Muhammad did the same. Similar claims were made for the Buddha.

[80] This story may be found in the *Infancy Gospel of Thomas* 2:1-5.

[81] The Latin *Gospel of Thomas* 7:1-2 (not to be confused with the other so-called *Gospel of Thomas* [c.180 AD]).

[82] See 37:102.

[83] However, there is another possibility. Some Muslims consider Abraham's father to be *Tarakh* (a very similar word to *Terah*, which is *Tarakh* in the Hebrew Old Testament), and Eusebius, the fourth-century church historian, refers to *Tarah* as *Athar* (a word very similar to Azar).

[84] Muslim apologists sometimes say that the stones were volcanic in origin. This is an attempt to harmonize the Qur'an with the biblical account, which specifies "brimstone [sulfur] and fire" ("burning sulfur" in the NIV) as falling from the sky and incinerating the cities of Sodom, Gomorrah (Genesis 19).

[85] Others think it may have been Alexander the Great (d. 323 BC). The identity of the traveler is not clear in this passage.

[86] One "difficulty" many claim to find in the Qur'an relates to the creation of man. In sura 23, we read that man was made from a clot of blood: "Then we made the sperm into a clot of congealed blood. Then, from that clot, we made a lump and we made out of that lump bones and clothed the bones with flesh" (23:13-14). In other words, the Qur'an has Adam being made from more recognizable biological material, while the Bible has him being made from clay (dirt). The biblical account seems to be more impressive. But this argument against the Muslim scriptures does not work. The Qur'an also describes man as having been created from clay: 15:26; 16:4;

22:5; 23:12-14; 40:67. The truth is, biblical and Qur'anic accounts alike are figurative. Neither account necessarily contradicts modern science, unless it is unnaturally forced into a literal interpretation. For more on this, see Paul Copan and Douglas Jacoby, *Origins: The Ancient Impact and Modern Implications of Genesis 1-11* (New York: NY, Morgan James), 2018.

[87] *The Satanic Verses: A Novel* (New York: St. Martin's Press, 1988).

[88] 15:87 refers to the lines of the first sura: "And certainly We have given thee seven oft-repeated (verses) and the grand Qur'an."

[89] The Jewish Apocrypha are works written in the "Intertestamental period," ranging from 400 BC to nearly the time of Christ. They bridge the gap between the testaments.

[90] The Arabic word for gospel, *Injil*, comes from the Latin evangelium, which in turn comes from the original Greek *euangelion*.

[91] 5:14,66,68 are interpreted as saying that the Bible had been changed. And yet the Quranic charge is that the biblical message had been forgotten (disobeyed), not transformed into something no longer true. Further, Muslims sometimes offer the Gospel of Barnabas in evidence of their position. Yet this forgery appeared no earlier than the 15th century, nor is there any earlier mention of it in Christian history. Here Jesus is "Christ," but not "Messiah" (!). The Jubilee occurs every 100 years—and yet the Vatican had changed it from every 50 years only in 1343. There are other anachronisms as well.

[92] The charge that the Christians adulterated the Scriptures by changing the *meaning* of the text (as opposed to tampering with the manuscripts) is found in suras 2, 3, and 4. This is called *Tahrif*.

[93] This is the John Rylands fragment, or p52, which contains part of chapter 18 of John's gospel.

[94] Some scrolls from the sixth century BC have also been discovered, but this represents a very small fraction of Old Testament scripture.

[95] Occasionally a scribe would try to "correct" or improve the text, but the sheer number of manuscripts makes it virtually impossible for such "improvements" to stand up under the scrutiny of Textual Criticism. (Textual Criticism is the science of reconstructing the original test by comparing the many manuscripts and manuscript families. For more on this, see Bruce M. Metzger, *The Text of the New Testament, 4th Edition* (Oxford: Oxford University Press, 2005).

[96] Microfilm versions of these manuscripts became available in 1997.

[97] For more on this, go to http://www.answering-islam.org/Campbell/s3c3b.html.

[98] *The People of the Mosque* (London: Student Christian Movement

Press, 1932), 62.

[99] See the Appendix for more than a hundred resources for further study. For more on the textual transmission of the Qur'an, see http:// www.islamic-awareness.org/Quran/Text/Mss/.

[100] This is an acronym. The *t* comes from *torah* (law), *n* from *nevi'im* (prophets), and *kh* from *khetuwim* (writings). These are the three sections of the Jewish Bible.

[101] *Mishnah* is the Hebrew word for "repetition"; the oral law repeated and amplified the written (Mosaic) law.

[102] For a quick overview of the Hadith, I have recorded three podcasts (with notes): Islam C (hadith part 1), https://www.douglasjacoby. com/had1/, Islam D (hadith part 2), https://www.douglasjacoby. com/had2/, and Islam E (hadith part 3), https://www.douglasjacoby. com/had3/.

[103] This is based on sura 2:106: "If we abrogate a verse or consign it to oblivion, we offer something better than it or something of equal value."

[104] Some Muslims insist the tomb of Jesus Christ is in Kashmir!

[105] SAt least 50% of Muslims in lands like Morocco, Turkey, Malaysia, Pakistan, and the Palestinian Territories believe the return of Christ will happen in their lifetime. (In contrast, a 2015 poll by the Brookings Institute found that only 12% of evangelical Christians believe Jesus will return in their lifetime.) He will descend to the earth, witness against Christians who believe he is the "Son of God," kill all pigs, break the crosses, go on hajj, defeat the Christian armies of Rome—the final battle to take place in Dabiq (Syria) or else Amaq (Turkey), kill the Antichrist, and usher in a period of worldwide Islamic prosperity.

[106] Malachi 4:2.

Chapter Four—Violence

[107] No sooner had the terror attacks passed, than the DC Beltway Snipers were upon us. John Muhammad and Lee Malvo had all of metro Washington on alert. Their indiscriminate killing spree was a different genre of terror, only seemingly "Muslim" thanks to Muhammad's name. We could not pick up our children from school unless we actually went into the school and escorted them out personally. For weeks, schools would not even allow the children to walk across parking lots. It was exhausting, it was a nuisance, and even though we knew our chances of being shot were very small, fear was everywhere.

[108] An example is the following alarmist piece, circulated on the

World Wide Web, with the preface:

"This study is most interesting. This is a serious matter. Be afraid—very afraid! Islam is not just a religion, nor is it a cult. In its fullest form... it is a complete, total, 100% system of life. Islam has religious, legal, political, economic, social, and military components. The religious component is a beard for all of the other components. Islamization begins when there are sufficient Muslims in a country to agitate for their religious privileges. When politically correct, tolerant, and culturally diverse societies agree to Muslim demands for their religious privileges, some of the other components tend to creep in as well. Here's how it works.

As long as the Muslim population remains around or under 2% in any given country, they will for the most part be regarded as a peace-loving minority, and not as a threat to other citizens. This is the case in: United States – 0.6% Muslim, Australia –1.5%, Canada – 1.9%, China – 1.8%, Italy – 1.5%, Norway – 1.8%. At 2% to 5%, they begin to proselytize other ethnic minorities and disaffected groups, often with major recruiting from the jails and among street gangs. This is happening in: Denmark – 2%, Germany – 3.7%, United Kingdom – 2.7%, Spain – 4%, Thailand – 4.6%. From 5% on, they exercise an inordinate influence in proportion to their percentage of the population. For example, they will push for the introduction of *halal* (clean by Islamic standards) food, thereby securing food preparation jobs for Muslims. They will increase pressure on supermarket chains to feature *halal* on their shelves—along with threats for failure to comply. This is occurring in: France – 8%, Philippines – 5%, Sweden – 5%, Switzerland – 4.3%, the Netherlands – 5.5%, Trinidad & Tobago – 5.8%. At this point, they will work to get the ruling government to allow them to rule themselves (within their ghettos) under *Shari'a*, the Islamic Law. The ultimate goal of Islamists is to establish *Shari'a* law over the entire world. When Muslims approach 10% of the population, they tend to increase lawlessness as a means of complaint about their conditions. In Paris we are already seeing car-burnings. Any non-Muslim action offends Islam, and results in uprisings and threats, such as in Amsterdam, with opposition to Mohammed cartoons and films about Islam. Such tensions are seen daily, particularly in Muslim sections, in: Guyana – 10%, India – 13.4%, Israel – 16%, Kenya – 10%, Russia – 15%.

After reaching 20%, nations can expect hair-trigger rioting, jihad militia formations, sporadic killings, and the burnings of Christian churches and Jewish synagogues, such as in: Ethiopia – 32.8%. At 40%, nations experience widespread massacres, chronic terror attacks, and ongoing militia warfare, such as in: Bosnia – 40%, Chad – 53.1%, Lebanon – 59.7%. From 60%, nations experience unfettered persecution of non-believers of all other religions (including non-conforming Muslims), sporadic ethnic cleansing (genocide), use of *Shari'a Law* as a weapon, and Jizya, the tax placed on infidels, such as in: Albania – 70%, Malaysia – 60.4%, Qatar – 77.5%, Sudan – 70%.

After 80%, expect daily intimidation and violent jihad, some State-run ethnic cleansing, and even some genocide, as these nations drive out the infidels, and move toward 100% Muslim, such as has been experienced and in some ways is ongoing in: Bangladesh – 83%, Egypt – 90%, Gaza – 98.7%, Indonesia – 86.1%, Iran – 98%, Iraq – 97%, Jordan – 92%, Morocco – 98.7%, Pakistan – 97%, Palestine – 99%, Syria – 90%, Tajikistan – 90%, Turkey – 99.8%, United Arab Emirates – 96%.

100% will usher in the peace of "Dar-es-Salaam"—the Islamic House of Peace. Here there's supposed to be peace, because everybody is a Muslim, the *madrassas* are the only schools, and the Koran is the only word, such as in: Afghanistan – 100%, Saudi Arabia – 100%, Somalia – 100%, Yemen – 100%. Unfortunately, peace is never achieved, as in these 100% states the most radical Muslims intimidate and spew hatred, and satisfy their blood lust, by killing less radical Muslims for a variety of reasons...

It is important to understand that in some countries, with well under 100% Muslim populations, such as France, the minority Muslim populations live in ghettos, within which they are 100% Muslim, and within which they live by *Shari'a* Law. The national police do not even enter these ghettos. There are no national courts or schools or non-Muslim religious facilities. In such situations, Muslims do not integrate into the community at large. The children attend madrassas. They learn only the Koran. To convert to, or even associate with, an infidel is a crime punishable with death. Therefore, in some areas of certain nations, Imams and extremists exercise more power than the national average would indicate. Today's 1.5 billion Muslims make up 22% of the world's population. But their birth rates dwarf the birth rates of Christians, Hindus, Buddhists, and Jews, and all other believers. Muslims will exceed 50% of the world's population by the end of this century." Adapted from Dr. Peter Hammond, *Slavery, Terrorism and Islam: The Historical Roots and Contemporary Threat* (Capetown: Christian Liberty Books, 2005).

While the correlations noted are indisputable, the directionality and complexities of causation are not adequately accounted for. Could it not be that societies with strong proclivities for totalitarianism attract radical Islam, radical Hinduism, etc?

[109] *Abraham: A Journey to the Heart of Three Faiths* (New York: William Morrow, 2002), 213.

[110] Sam Harris, *The End of Faith: Religion, Terror, and the Future of Reason* (New York: W.W. Norton, 2004), 129.

[111] In Afghanistan, a homosexual would typically be forced to stand behind a wall, and then a tank would push the wall on top of him and crush him to death—burying him alive. Source: Baker, Barbara B. "Afghanistan: Taliban Threatens Converts," *Christianity Today* online (March 5, 2001), www.christianitytoday.com/ct/2001/march5/22.34.html.

[112] *Christianity Today* (January, 2001).

[113] And why doesn't the United States challenge its ally to update its law codes, bringing them into the twenty-first century? Presumably access to oil is more important to US economic interests than human rights. A strong verdict, but how else can the evidence be interpreted?

[114] "A British teacher jailed for naming a teddy bear Mohammed on Monday said she is 'sad to be leaving Sudan' after being granted a full presidential pardon... In a written statement, the 54-year-old mother of two [Gillian Gibbons] said she was sorry if she had caused distress and added that she had "great respect" for Islam... Gibbons was convicted of insulting Islam at the end of an eight-hour hearing... and sentenced to 15 days in detention. She had faced 40 lashes or up to a year in prison." Source: From *Al Bawaba*, 3 December 2007, http://www.albawaba.com/en/countries/Sudan/219543.

[115] "...The sentence against the 19-year-old Shia woman from Qatif... was passed because she was in the car of a man who was not a relative at the time of the attack, which contravened strict Saudi laws on segregation... According to the Arab News newspaper, the woman was gang-raped 14 times. Her offence was in meeting a former boyfriend, whom she had asked to return pictures he had of her because she was about to marry another man. The couple was sitting in a car when a group of seven Sunni men kidnapped them and raped them both, lawyers in the case told Arab News. The former boyfriend was also sentenced to 90 lashes... The victims' lawyer, Abdul-Rahman al-Lahem, was also ordered to face disciplinary action after he spoke to the media... 'My client is the victim of this abhorrent crime. I believe her sentence contravenes the Islamic Shari'a law and violates the pertinent international conventions,' he said. 'The judicial bodies should have dealt with this girl as the victim rather than the culprit. The court blamed the girl for being alone with unrelated men, but it should have taken the humane view that it cannot be considered her

fault.' The crime of rape can carry the death penalty in Saudi Arabia."
Source: http://ww4report.com/node/4675/print.

Another example—and they are many!—comes from 2008,
as reported in Voice of the Martyrs: "Mansuur Mohammed (25), a
charity worker who converted from Islam to Christianity in 2005,
was beheaded by Islamists on September 23 in Manyafulka village,
according to an October 27 report from Compass Direct. Mohammed
and a fellow World Food Program worker were driving when their
vehicle was intercepted by members of the *al Shabab* Islamist militant
group. The driver managed to flee the scene but Mohammed was
captured. In the afternoon, the militants gathered the villagers by
telling them that they were going to prepare a feast for them. Five
masked men armed with guns and swords dragged the handcuffed
Mohammed in front of the crowd. One militant recited the Qur'an as
he proclaimed Mohammed a *murtid* (an Arabic term for an apostate
who leaves Islam) and also claimed that he was a spy for Ethiopian
soldiers. The militants, chanting *Allahu Akbar* (God is great), then
beheaded Mohammed and cheered while holding up his severed
head in front of the horrified crowd. A video of the murder was later
circulated in Somalia and in neighbouring countries in what many
see as an effort to instill fear in those contemplating converting from
Islam to Christianity. Mohammed's martyrdom is the latest in a wave
of such attacks on Christians in Somalia in recent months."

An Associated Press article from Kabul, Afghanistan (6 February
2009) reported the imprisonment of six Afghans for translating the
Qur'an from Arabic into a local language. Not only did they fail to
include the Arabic text with the translation (page by page), but they
even brought the document into a mosque, whose cleric had printed
one thousand copies of the book for them. The establishment, offended
by this allegedly irreverent act accused the project leader, Zalmai, of
"modifying the Qur'an." He is considered an infidel.

The prosecutor is pushing for the death penalty. As the AP article
relates, "Sentences on religious infractions can be harsh. In January
2008, a court sentenced a journalism student to death for blasphemy
for asking questions about women's rights under Islam. An appeals
court reduced the sentence to 20 years in prison. His lawyers appealed
again and the case is pending. In 2006, an Afghan man was sentenced
to death for converting to Christianity. He was later ruled insane and
was given asylum in Italy. Islamic leaders and the parliament accused
President Hamid Karzai of being a puppet for the West for letting him
live. Nooristani, who is also defending the journalism student, said he
and his colleagues have received death threats. 'The mullahs in the

mosques have said whoever defends an infidel is an infidel...'"

Hundreds, and probably thousands, of other examples have come to my attention as I have studied Islam in current events. Freedom of religion is rarer in the Muslim world than most Muslims care to admit.

[116] "The Saudi Ministry of Islamic Affairs, Endowment, Call and Guidance employs 120,000 people, including 72,000 imams. Saudi Arabia bans non-Islamic worship and regards attempts to convert Muslims to another faith as a criminal offence." Source: "The battle of the books," Dec 19th 2007 | Washington DC. From *The Economist* print edition. Copyright © 2008 The Economist Newspaper and The Economist Group. All rights reserved.

[117] Research shows that those who carry out honor killings tend to be the less-observant Muslims: men with criminal records, from broken homes. In other words, it is not their faith that is driving them to kill family members, but social expectations.

[118] This saying is not part of any of the authoritative Hadith collections. Traditionally it is attributed to Ibrahim ibn Ablah, according to Nisa'i in al-Kuna.

[119] Suicide bombing is only a few decades old. E.g., there was not a single suicide bombing in the Soviet-Afghan War.

[120] On the other hand, to be fair, in sub-Saharan Africa, Malaysia, and Indonesia, the faith was spread by peaceful means.

[121] Kennedy, John W. "Finding Homes for the Lost Boys," *Christianity Today* magazine online (July 8, 2001).

[122] Some of the more helpful websites are www.persecution.com, www.christianitytoday.com, and www.gmi.org/ow. An example of a recent story of martyrdom is "Tortured to Death," by Jeff M. Sellers of Compass Direct, who relates the death on 5 September 2007 of an Eritrean woman who refused to deny her faith at the hands of her Muslim captors. Source: http://www.christianitytoday.com/ct/2007/december/2.15.html.

A high estimate is 465 Christians martyred worldwide on a daily basis. Source: http://www.gospelweb.net/modmartyrsindex2.htm.

[123] Hinduism, the great religion of tolerance, ironically also harbors a violent side. In parts of India, Christianity is brutally suppressed and people have been killed, burned to death. In 2009, the going price on a pastor's head is $250, making Christian ministry dangerous work in places such as Orissa state.

[124] These are mainly the nations of the (Asian) Middle East, as well as the African nations of Morocco, the Sudan, Nigeria, Ethiopia, Eritrea, and Egypt. Moreover, there are approximately 75 nations

that persecute religious believers, primarily Christians. The main offenders:

• *Muslim states.* The increasing application of shari'a law is creating multiplied opportunities for persecution. In some nations, courts sentence nationals to death for converting to Christianity. In most Muslim countries, relatives will sometimes murder those who come to believe in Christ. For example, in Egypt, Coptic Christians are often persecuted. Buildings and shops are burned or vandalized. Yet the government does little if anything to stop the violence, which parallels Hindu violence and sluggish governmental response in India.

• *Marxist states.* These nations continue to make life difficult for believers, especially in North Korea, where profession of faith leads to imprisonment and death. In China, Vietnam, and Laos, unregistered Christians may be imprisoned, tortured, executed, or sent to labor camp.

• *Hindu extremists.* Acts of terror often take place against believers in India and Nepal.

• *Buddhist persecutors.* Christians have been maltreated, especially in Bhutan and Sri Lanka.

[125] Richard Bulliet, *The Case for Islamo-Christian Civilization* (New York: Columbia University Press, 2004).

[126] For example, the Aryan Nations, Contras (Nicaragua), ETA (Euskadi Ta Askatasuna), Ku Klux Klan, Nagaland Rebels, Red Brigades, Ulster Volunteer Force, Tamil Tigers—and scores more! See http://en.wikipedia.org/wiki/List_of_terrorist_organisations#_note-MIPT.

[127] To resort to a lighthearted example, it would be like trying to explain to a fish, "You are all wet. You only experience water, you do not know what the world is like." I guess a fish, if he could talk, might reply, "Yeah, of course, water is everywhere. What else is there?" He does not have the experience of being on the land or being in the sky. Water is his element. He is used to it, he is comfortable in it.

[128] I offer a thorough discussion of parenting in Western culture in my book, *Principle-Centered Parenting* (Spring, TX: Illumination Publishers International, 2015).

[129] See Matthew 6:19: "Do not store up for yourselves treasures on earth," and Matthew 6:24: "You cannot serve both God and Money."

[130] To be fair, a large percentage of US oil imports are not from the Middle East at all. Such nations as Nigeria, Venezuela, Canada and Mexico are major exporters to the US. According to the Energy Information Administration, the top five countries for crude oil and petroleum imports into the United States are, in order, Canada, Saudi

Arabia, Mexico, Venezuela, and Nigeria, with only three other Middle Eastern nations in the top fifteen.

[131] This is known as the "verse of the sword."

[132] The context of this passage is Muhammad dealing with his Meccan opponents.

[133] In sura 26:49, Pharaoh threatens cutting off hands on opposite sides of the body and crucifixion as a threat to Moses. See also 12:41 and 20:71. And yet is there any evidence that ancient Egyptians practiced crucifixion? Crucifixion came into existence in the sixth century BC—far too late for Genesis. The fancy explanation at http://www.islamic-awareness.org/Quran/Contrad/External/crucify.html does not convince. (The word *impale* should have been used.)

[134] See http://www.thereligionofpeace.com/Qur'an/018-suicide-bombing.htm. The Hadith can be searched at www.usc.edu/dept/MSA/reference/searchhadith.html.

Chapter Five—Response

[135] It may be asked: Why, then, did Jesus seemingly tell his apostles to buy a sword (Luke 22:36)? The point seems to be that from this point on his disciples will be subject to persecution and danger. To paraphrase, "Be vigilant; you are going to need protection."

[136] Thanks to John Stewart of South Dakota for directing me to this vignette, and for his summary statement.

[137] All quotations are available in *The Antenicene Fathers.*

[138] Let me offer an illustration from my own denomination, the Churches of Christ. The Espionage Act of 1917 (the year the United States entered World War I) gave U.S. district attorneys the power to shut down pacifist publications, such as The Gospel Advocate. When D.A. Lee Douglas threatened the editor, J. C. McQuiddy, because of the pacifist articles in the Gospel Advocate, articles became pro-America and pro-war.

[139] See John Driver, *How Christians Made Peace with War* (Scottsdale, Pennsylvania: Herald Press, 1988). This explains exactly how the early church pacifist position became militaristic with the advent of the church state in the fourth century. Or read through all relevant quotations by studying David Berçot's *A Dictionary of Early Christian Beliefs* (Hendrickson, 1998).

[140] The website is http://myblessedhome.blogspot.com/2007/01/why-christians-need-to-support-war.html.

[141] The occasion was the First Jewish War (66–73 AD). Jesus is prophesying about the destruction of Jerusalem (70 AD).

[142] http://www.ptm.org/02PT/MayJun/war.htm.

[143] 2 Chronicles 32:8, Psalm 20:7, 1 Kings 3:1ff, and many other passages.

[144] The Iraqi War is not going well at the time of this writing (2008). As David Aikman astutely observes, tens of thousands of Christians are among the 2 million Iraqi refugees in Jordan and Syria. "It is one of the great unintended consequences of the war in Iraq that the U.S., a Christian-majority nation, led its military forces to liberate a Muslim nation, leading to a dramatic drop in religious freedom for this nation's Christian minority." Source: *Christianity Today* (December 2007), 58.

[145] Dietrich Bonhoeffer, John Stott, and David Berçot come to mind.

[146] See Greg Mortensen and David Relin's bestselling *Three Cups of Tea* (New York: Penguin, 2006). As Mortensen insightfully asks, "Now take the cost of one of those [Tomahawk] missiles tipped with a Raytheon guidance system, which I think is about $840,000. For that much money, you could build dozens of schools that could provide tens of thousands of students with a balanced non-extremist education over the course of a generation. Which do you think will make us more secure?" (294-295)

[147] See Ron Sider's superb article, "Courageous Nonviolence," in *Christianity Today* (December 2007), 44-45.

[148] Interestingly, according to a 2007 Gallup Poll, there were 156 anti-Islamic hate crimes reported in the United States during 2006. The number of anti-Jewish hate crimes was 967. One wonders, will anti-Islamic prejudice and crime rise to the ugly level of Anti-Semitism?

Chapter Six—Connections

[149] The Greek word *ethne* might better be translated *peoples,* given that *nations* has political connotations absent in biblical times.

[150] Hadith 2,562 in the Sunan al-Tirmidhi, which reads, "The least [reward] for the people of Heaven is 80,000 servants and 72 wives, over which stands a dome of pearls, aquamarine, and ruby."

[151] Robert Morey, *The Islamic Invasion* (Grand Rapids: Kregel, 1995). Though the book can be caustic at times, it does make a number of astute observations. On the other hand, it seems that *all* civilizations in the past engaged in "cultural imperialism," not just the Muslim and European Christian ones. The supreme irony is that, while Muslims accuse the West of imperialism—and I agree that there is more than of world coa modicum of truth in the allegation—the Muslim goal of world conquest certainly qualifies them as equally (if not more) imperialistic.

[152] In the Trinity, there is eternal love among the three persons.

Yet Allah is singular; there was no one to love before he created, and so he cannot be eternally loving, let alone love. In fairness, there is a tradition that "When God created the world, He wrote above his Throne, 'My mercy precedes My wrath'" (Hadith of Bukhari 22:55). Some Sufi Muslims claim that God is love and his love is eternal. (Seyyed Hossein Nasr, The Garden of Truth: The Vision and Promise of Sufism, Islam's Mystical Tradition [San Francisco, CA: HarperOne, 2007], 61), cited in Miroslav Volf, Allah: A Christian Response (New York, NY: HarperOne, 2011), p.294, n.10.

[153] Here James appears to be quoting from the apocryphal Sirach 5:11.

[154] The majority of Muslims believe that Jesus will descend from heaven on the wings of two angels, and then will invite the whole world to become Muslims, including Christians and Jews. He will then kill the one-eyed Antichrist, and slay seventy thousand Jews. Jesus will destroy the idolatrous symbol of the Cross, exterminate all swine, and end all wars. All other religions will end, and Islam will triumph.

[155] For example, Neil Lightfoot, *How We Got the Bible* (Grand Rapids: Baker, 1987) and even my own audio sets, *How We Got the Bible* (Spring, Texas: Illumination Publishers, 2005) and *The Lost Books of the Bible That Were Never Missing* (Spring, Texas: Illumination Publishers, 2007).

[156] E.g. Muhammad Abu Zahra (1898-1974), Sheikh Ahmed Hussein Deedat (1918-2005), and Shabir Ally (1962-), Guyanese-born professor at Saint Mary's University in Halifax, Nova Scotia.

[157] Rashad Khalifa, *The Final Testament Authorized English Version,* Translated from the Original (1992), 1.

[158] *On the Formation of the Foetus.* Galen of Pergamum lived 129-200 AD.

[159] Another example of spurious evidence is that Mecca is "aligned" with the magnetic north pole—for which reason the prime meridian ought to be redrawn through Saudi Arabia. Yet unlike the geographic north pole, magnetic north drifts; it is not a constant. In short, like some Christians, some Muslims err when they search their scriptures for scientific confirmation of the truth of their religion.

[160] They have confused *Teman* with *Tema.*

[161] Hamadi ibn Abdullah al-Buhri, *Uteni wa Sayedina Huseni,* quoted in Esposito, *Islam,* 112.

[162] The triumph of Mariolatry took place at the Council of Ephesus, 431 AD.

[163] Genesis 21:22; Deuteronomy 33:27; Psalm 119:89, 160; Micah

5:2; Matthew 24:35; John 8:58; Hebrews 13:8.

[164] Some would argue that the Qur'an is eternal in only one direction, that the *book* did not always exist, though its contents always existed. But if that is the case, it can easily be argued that the Qur'an is eternal.

[165] Norman Geisler and Abdul Saleeb. *Answering Islam: The Crescent in Light of the Cross* (Grand Rapids, Michigan: Baker, 1993).

[166] Yancey, Philip, "The Back Page: Letter from a Muslim Seeker," *Christianity Today*, vol. 45, no. 15 (December 3, 2001), 80. Used with permission from Philip Yancey.

Chapter Seven—Jesus and Muslims

[167] The Samarian Pentateuch combined the first and second commandments of Exodus 20, to leave room for one additional commandment. It said, in effect, "Thou shalt worship the Lord thy God on Mount Gerizim." Hence the dispute between the Jews and the Samaritans reflected in John 4:20. In fact, the Samaritans had even built their *own* temple atop this mountain. Though it was destroyed by John Hyrcanus in 129 BC, the remnant of the ancient Samaritans, several hundred in number, congregate there annually to celebrate the Passover.

[168] In the words of a Jewish apocryphal book, "There are two nations that my soul detests, the third is not a nation at all: the inhabitants of Mount Seir, the Philistines, and the stupid people living at Shechem" (Sirach 50:25-26 NJB).

[169] As we read in John 4:9c, "Jews, of course, do not associate with Samaritans."

[170] See, for example, Luke 9:52ff and John 8:48. And yet God always loved the Samaritans, and they were part of his plan; see Acts 1:8.

[171] For this insight I am indebted to Gordon Fee and Douglas Stuart, who made the point in *How to Read the Bible For All Its Worth* (Grand Rapids: Zondervan, 2003), 160-161.

[172] In 2 Kings 1, Elijah called down fire from heaven to consume those who were opposing him.

[173] "That (is so). And whoever retaliates with the like of that with which he if afflicted and he is oppressed, Allah will certainly help him... (22:60). "Whoever transgresses against you, respond in kind" (2:194).

Bibliography:
Resources for Further Study

Books

General

Accad, Fouad Elias, *Building Bridges: Christianity and Islam.* Colorado Springs, Colo.: NavPress, 1997.

Adeney, Miriam, *Daughters of Islam: Building Bridges with Muslim Women.* Downers Grove, Ill.: InterVarsity, 2002.

Alam, Christopher, *Out of Islam: One Muslim's Journey of Faith in Christ.* Somerville, Mass.: Frontline, 2006.

Anderson, J. Kerby, *A Biblical Point of View on Islam.* Eugene, Ore.: Harvest House, 2008.

Armstrong, Karen, *Islam (A Short History).* New York: Random House, 2002.

Aslan, Reza, *No god but God: The Origins, Evolution and Future of Islam.* New York: Random House, 2005.

Belt, Don, ed., *The World of Islam.* New York: Random House, 2001.

Bergen, Peter L., *Holy War, Inc.* New York: Simon & Schuster, 2002.

Braswell, George W., Jr., *Islam.* Nashville, Tenn.: Broadman & Holman, 1996.

Caner, Ergun Mehmet, *Unveiling Islam: An Insider's Look at Muslim Life and Beliefs.* Grand Rapids, Mich.: Kregel, 2002.

Cavendish, Richard, *The Great Religions.* London: W. H. Smith, 1980.

Chandler, Paul-Gordon. *Pilgrims of Christ on the Muslim Road: Exploring a New Path between Two Faiths.* Lanham, Md.: Rowman & Littlefield Publishers, Inc. 2008

Chapman, Colin, *Cross and Crescent: Responding to the Challenge of Islam.* Downers Grove, Ill.: InterVarsity, 2003.

____. *Islam and the West.* Colorado Springs, Colo.: Authentic, 1998.

Clark, Malcolm, *Islam for Dummies.* Hoboken, N.J.: John Wiley & Sons, 2003.

Cook, Michael, *Muhammad.* Oxford: Oxford University Press, 1983.

Coplestone, F. S., *Jesus Christ or Mohammed? A Guide to Islam and Christianity.* Ross-shire, Scotland, U.K.: Christian Focus Publications, 2000.

Cragg, Kenneth, *The Call of the Minaret.* Maryknoll, N.Y.: Orbis, 1985.

Dedat, Ahmad, *Islamic Selections.* Mecca: Muslim World League, 1983.

Edis, Taner, *An Illusion of Harmony: Science and Religion in Islam.* Amherst, N.Y.: Prometheus Books, 2007.

Eerdman's Handbook to The World's Religions. Grand Rapids, Mich.: Eerdmans, 1992.

Elias, Jamal, ed. by Ninian Smart, *Islam.* Upper Saddle River, N.J.: Prentice Hall, 1999.

Esposito, John L., *The Oxford History of Islam.* Oxford: Oxford University Press, 1999.

Esposito, John L., and Dalia Mogahed, *"Who Speaks for Islam? What a Billion Muslims Really Think."* New York: Gallup Press, 2007.

Feiler, Bruce, Abraham: *A Journey to the Heart of Three Faiths.* New York: William Morrow, 2002.

Firestone, Reuven, *An Introduction to Islam for Jews.* Philadelphia: Jewish Publication Society, 2008.

Geisler, Norman, and Abdul Saleeb, *Answering Islam: The Crescent in Light of the Cross.* Grand Rapids, Mich.: Baker, 1993.

Goldmann, David, *Islam and the Bible: Why Two Faiths Collide.* Chicago: Moody, 2004.

Goldsmith, *What About Other Faiths?* London: Hodder & Stoughton, 1989.

Goodwin, Jan, *Price of Honor.* London: Little, Brown, 1994.

Haleem, M. A. S. Abdel. *The Qur'an: A New Translation.* Oxford: Oxford University Press, 2016.

Hassaballa, Hesham A., *The Beliefnet Guide to Islam.* New York: Random House, 2006.

Hewer, C. T. R., *Understanding Islam: An Introduction.* Minneapolis, Minn.: Augsburg Press, 2006.

Holland, Tom. *In the Shadow of the Sword: The Battle for Global Empire and the End of the Ancient World.* London: Abacus, 2012.

Hourani, Albert, *A History of the Arab Peoples.* Cambridge, Mass.: Harvard University Press, 1991.

Iqbal, Muzaffar, *Science and Islam.* Westport, Conn.: Greenwood Press, 2007.

Kaltner, John, *Islam: What Non-Muslims Should Know*. Minneapolis, Minn.: Augsburg Press, 2003.

Lewis, Bernard, *Islam: From the Prophet Muhammad to the Capture of Constantinople*. Oxford: Oxford University Press, 1987.

Lippman, Thomas W., *Understanding Islam: An Introduction to the Muslim World*. New York: Meridian, 1995.

Love, Rick, *Muslims, Magic, and the Kingdom of God*. Pasadena, Calif.: William Carey, 2001.

Mahmud, Sayyid F., *Short History of Islam*. Oxford: Oxford University Press, 1989.

Malone, Henry, *Islam Unmasked*. Irving, Tex,: Vision Life, 2002.

Marshall, Paul, ed., *Religious Freedom in the World*. Nashville, Tenn.: Broadman & Holman, 2000.

McAuliffe, Jane Damme, ed., *The Cambridge Companion to the Qur'an*. Cambridge, England, U.K.: Cambridge University Press, 2006.

McDermott, Gerald R., *Can Evangelicals Learn from World Religions? Jesus, Revelation & Religious Traditions*. Downers Grove, Ill.: Inter-Varsity, 2000.

Meddeb, Abdelwahab, *The Malady of Islam*. Philadelphia: Running Press, 2002.

Mernissi, Fatima, *The Veil and Male Elite*. New York: Addison-Wesley, 1991.

Mortensen, Greg, and David Oliver Relin, *Three Cups of Tea*. New York: Penguin, 2006.

Musk, Bill, *The Unseen Face of Islam*. Grand Rapids, Mich.: Kregel, 2004.

Nasr, Seyyed, ed., *Islamic Spirituality: Manifestations*. Norwich, England, U.K.: SCM–Canterbury Press Limited, 1991.

Parshall, Phil, *Bridges to Islam.* Colorado Springs, Colo.: Authentic, 2007.

Patterson, Margot, *Islam Considered: A Christian View.* Collegeville, Minn.: Liturgical Press, 2008.

Peters, F. E., *Muhammad and the Origins of Islam.* Albany, N.Y.: SUNY Press, 1994.

Rahman, Fazlur, *Islam.* Chicago: University of Chicago Press, 1979.

Rhodes, Ron, *Islam: What You Need to Know.* Irvine, Tex.: Harvest House, 2000.

Riddell, Peter G. and Peter Coterrell, *Islam in Context: Past, Present and Future.* Grand Rapids, Mich.: Baker, 2003.

Rippin, Andrew, *Muslims.* New York: Routledge, 2000.

Ruthven, Malise, and Azim Nanji, *Historical Atlas of Islam.* Cambridge, Mass.: Harvard University Press, 2004.

Ruthven, Malise, *Islam: A Very Short Introduction.* Oxford: Oxford University Press, 2000.

Safa, Reza F., *Inside Islam.* Lake Mary, Fla.: Strang Communications, 1996.

Sardar, Ziauddin, *What Do Muslims Believe: The Roots and Realities of Modern Islam.* New York: Walker and Company, 2007.

Schulze, Reinhard, *A Modern History of the Islamic World.* New York: NYU Press, 2000.

Shipp, Glover, *Christianity and Islam: Bridging Two Worlds.* Webb City, Mo.: Covenant Publishing, 2002.

Sire, James W., *The Universe Next Door: A Basic Worldview Catalog.* Downers Grove, Ill.: InterVarsity, 1997.

Smith, Huston, *Islam.* San Francisco: Harper, 2001.

Sonn, Tamara, *A Brief History of Islam*. Hoboken, N.J.: Blackwell, 2004.

Sultan, Wafa. *A God Who Hates: The Courageous Woman Who Inflamed the Muslim World Speaks Out Against the Evils of Islam*. New York, NY: St. Martin's Press, 2009.

Swartley, Keith E., ed., *Encountering the World of Islam*. Colorado Springs, Colo.: Authentic, 2005.

Tsoukalas, Steven, *The Nation of Islam*. Somerville, Mass.: Frontline, 2001.

Volf, Miroslav. *Allah: A Christian Response*. New York, NY: HarperOne, 2011.

Watt, W. Montgomery, *Muhammad: Prophet and Statesman*. Oxford: Oxford University Press, 1961.

Zacharias, Ravi, *Jesus Among Other Gods: The Absolute Claims of the Christian Message*. Nashville, Tenn.: Word, 2000.

Zaka, Anees, and Diane Coleman, *The Truth about Islam: The Noble Qur'an's Teachings in Light of the Holy Bible*. Phillipsburg, N.J.: P & R Publishing, 2004.

Political Islam: Jihad, Militant Islam and Terrorism

Bard, Mitchell, *Myths and Facts*. Chevy Chase, Md.: AICE, 2001.

Byman, Daniel, *Deadly Connections: States that Sponsor Terrorism*. Oxford: Oxford University Press, 2007.

Fregosi, Paul, *Jihad in the West*. Amherst, N.Y.: Prometheus, 1998.

Friedman, Thomas, *From Beirut to Jerusalem*. New York: Farrar Straus & Giroux, 1989.

Gabriel, Mark A., *Islam and Terrorism: What the Quran Really Teaches About Christianity, Violence and the Goals of Islamic Jihad*. Somerville, Mass.: Frontline, 2002.

Gartenstein-Ross, Daveed, *My Year Inside Radical Islam*. New York: Tarcher, 2008.

Grossman, David, *The Yellow Wind*. New York: Farrar Straus & Giroux, 1988.

Hammond, Peter, *Slavery, Terrorism and Islam: The Historical Roots and Contemporary Threat*. Capetown, South Africa: Christian Liberty Books, 2005.

Harris, Sam, *The End of Faith: Religion, Terror, and the Future of Reason*. New York: W.W. Norton, 2004.

Hitchens, Christopher, *God is Not Great: How Religion Poisons Everything*. New York: Twelve, 2007.

Jones, James W., *Blood that Cries from the Earth: The Psychology of Religious Terrorism*. Oxford: Oxford University Press, 2008.

Makiya, Kanan, *Cruelty and Silence*. New York: W. W. Norton, 1993.

Mamdani, Mahmood, *Good Muslim, Bad Muslim: America, the Cold War, and the Roots of Terror*. New York: Doubleday, 2005.

Man, John. *Saladin: The Life, The Legend and the Islamic Empire*. London: Corgi, 2015.

Masood, Steven, *Into the Light: A Young Muslim's Search for Truth*. Eastbourne, England, U.K.: Kingsway, 1986.

Miller, Judith, *God Has Ninety-Nine Names*. New York: Simon & Schuster, 1996.

Morey, Robert, *Islamic Invasion*. Grand Rapids, Mich.: Kregel, 1995.

Rashid, Ahmed, *Taliban*. New Haven, Conn.: Yale University Press, 2000.

Schwartz, Stephen, *The Two Faces of Islam: Saudi Fundamentalism and Its Role in Terrorism*. New York: Random House, 2003.

Shorrosh, Anis, *Islam Revealed: A Christian Arab's View of Islam*. Nashville, Tenn.: Thomas Nelson, 2001.

Sider, Ronald J. *Nonviolent Action: What Christian Ethics Demand but Most Christians Have Never Really Tried* (Grand Rapids, Mich: Brazos Press, 2015).

Spencer, Robert, *Islam Unveiled: Disturbing Questions about the World's Fastest-Growing Faith.* New York: Encounter Books, 2003.

Sproul, R. C., and Abdul Saleeb, *The Dark Side of Islam.* Wheaton, Ill.: Crossway, 2003.

Taylor, Aaron. D. *Alone with a Jihadist: A Biblical Response to Holy War.* Manchester, Conn: Foghorn Publishers, 2009.

Wagner, William, *How Islam Plans to Change the World.* Grand Rapids, Mich.: Kregel, 2004.

Weigel, George. *Faith, Reason, and the War Against Jihadism: A Call to Action.* New York: Doubleday, 2007.

Web and Other Resources

101 Cleared Up Contradictions of the Bible (responses to Muslim charges against the Bible)
http://debate.org.uk/topics/apolog/contrads.htm

Al-Muhaddith (download Qur'an, Hadith, legal material)
http://www.muhaddith.org

Al-Islam.org (introductory)
www.al-islam.org/

Answering Islam (hundreds of links)
http://www.answering-islam.org.uk

Apostates of Islam
http://apostatesofislam.com

Beliefnet (good general information)
http://www.beliefnet.com/index/index_10004.html

Biblical Training: Islam, with Timothy Tennent
http://www.biblicaltraining.org/class.php?class=WM647

Compass Direct News (News from the frontlines of persecution)
http://www.compassdirect.org/en/display.php

Compendium of Muslim Texts (University of Southern California)
http://www.usc.edu/dept/MSA/reference/searchhadith.html

Focus on Persecution (Ministering to Persecuted Christians Around the World)
http://www.focusonpersecution.com/Home.html

Free Koran (Free copies of the Qur'an through this site)
http://freekoran.com

Interview with Muslim Terrorist Recruiter
http://www.cbsnews.com/stories/2007/03/23/60minutes/main2602308.shtml

Islam 101 (an educational site on Islam, its lifestyle, civizilation, and culture)
http://www.islamfortoday.com

Islam.com (Muslim site)
http://www.islam.com/islamcateg.asp?index1=1&index2=13&index3=13

Islam for Today (promotes the theology of Islam)
http://www.islamfortoday.com

Islamic Gateway (great graphics and well organized)
http://www.ummah.org.uk

Islamicity (evangelistic site)
http://www.islam.org, www.islamicity.com

Islam and Islamic Studies (Professor Alan Godlas)
http://www.arches.uga.edu/~godlas

Islam World (Muslim site)
http://www.islamworld.net

Journey through Islam, with Erwun Caner
http://www.leestrobel.com/videos/Helping/CCNT1460.htm

Lessons from Muslims who have become Christians
http://www.leestrobel.com/videos/Helping/CCNT1460.htm

Mamalist of Islamic Links (more than 1000 links)
http://www.jannah.org/mamlist

Musalman: the Islamic Portal (good news coverage)
http://www.musalman.com

The Muslim-Christian Debate (intellectual and historical critique of Islam by Jay Smith)
http://www.debate.org.uk

Muttaqun OnLine: The Noble Quran
http://muttaqun.com/quran/e/

Operation World (global evangelism website)
http://www.gmi.org/ow

Persecution of Christians Under Islam
http://www.islam-on-line.org

Persecution.Org (persecution of Christians under Muslims)
http://www.persecution.org/suffering/index.php

Religious Tolerance (good general resource)
http://www.religioustolerance.org/islam.htm

Skeptics' Annotated Bible
http://www.skepticsannotatedbible.com/quran/contra/abrogation.html

Submission.org
http://submission.org

Voice of the Martyrs (persecuted Christians)
http://www.persecution.com

The World of Islam, CD (Global Mapping International, 2001)
http://www.gmi.org

www.ingramcontent.com/pod-product-compliance
Lightning Source LLC
Chambersburg PA
CBHW021623120626
46545CB00001B/370